Beyond the
Marriage Fantasy

Beyond the Marriage Fantasy

HOW TO ACHIEVE TRUE MARITAL INTIMACY

Daniel Beaver

Harper & Row, Publishers, San Francisco
Cambridge, Hagerstown, New York, Philadelphia
London, Mexico City, São Paulo, Sydney

1817

FIRST HARPER & ROW EDITION PUBLISHED IN 1983.

Designer: Jim Mennick

Library of Congress Cataloging in Publication Data

Beaver, Daniel.
  BEYOND THE MARRIAGE FANTASY.

  Rev. ed. of: The marriage fantasy. c1982.
  Bibliography: p. 185
  1. Marriage—Psychological aspects. I. Title.
HQ734.B46   1983   646.7′8   82-48918
ISBN 0-06-250051-1

---

83 84 85 86 87 10 9 8 7 6 5 4 3 2 1

For my wife, Debra

In memory of my father,
RICHARD DAVID BEAVER,

and my grandparents,
JOSEPH AND ROSE ROSE

Contents

Preface

Everyone who is planning on entering into marriage, or who has already done so, has a mental picture, with its corresponding expectations, of what will make that experience satisfying. *Beyond the Marriage Fantasy* explores our culture's common marital expectations. It looks at how they developed and their effect on our daily lives. As you read this book, you will become acutely aware of the myths and behavioral patterns that can frustrate your efforts to build a rewarding marriage.

One basic marital expectation that people share in our culture is the desire to have a satisfying, long-lasting relationship. But where, within our culture, are we taught in any straightforward way how to achieve this type of relationship? The attitude in this society seems to be that "if both spouses love each other, things will just work out naturally." There is a tremendous need for practical information about how to make and keep a marriage intimate and alive. Our divorce rate has reached a level that places an almost intolerable strain on society as a whole and, of course, on the growing number of affected individuals. Recent social and economic conditions have placed new demands on the institution of marriage. Our old marriage fantasy is no longer working for large numbers of people.

Beyond the Marriage Fantasy is a guide for those who are trailblazing the new frontier that the institution of marriage is entering. It provides practical information about marriage and the marital relationship that will help people see the changes they can make in response to those new demands. The reader will receive straightforward guidelines and tools for breaking with the old and creating a new, real intimacy in a marriage that is vital and alive for both partners. The main vehicle for attaining this goal is intimate verbal communication, which is a major topic of the book.

I have developed the material presented in this book through an evolutionary process that has included all the lectures, marital and individual therapy sessions, and classes I have conducted. My emphasis is not on what is "right" or "wrong" in a marital relationship, but on what works. *Beyond the Marriage Fantasy* is the synthesis of what has worked for me both personally and with hundreds of couples in the course of my professional career. I hope that, through this book I can help many more people see that having a long-lasting, intimate marriage is not just a romantic fantasy.

Examples used in this book are based on actual situations I've encountered in counseling, but in some instances the cases described are composites of several actual cases and in all cases the names and details about each person have been changed.

DANIEL BEAVER

Part I
Marriage in Crisis:
How We Got There

1. The Marriage Fantasy: A Key in the Crisis

As a marriage counselor in the San Francisco Bay Area, I have noticed a pattern among couples who come to my office seeking ways to save their marriages. In one respect, they are all very successful in their roles as husbands and wives. In fact, it is their success—a certain kind of success—that is at the center of their troubles.

More often than not, the husband and wife are succeeding at doing everything that their parents, their friends, and their culture teach are the *right* things to do to be a good wife or a good husband. But in spite of their well-meaning efforts, their marriages are failing. They describe the tension, frustration, and resentment they experience each day. And, as if that weren't enough, there is disappointment, sadness, and bewilderment.

Often a couple's disillusionment comes to the surface after about ten years of marriage. For the sake of discussion, let's take a couple we'll call Nick and Donna Stevens. They are thirty-two years old and have an upper middle-class income. To outsiders, the Stevenses look good. But something Nick and Donna can't quite identify is missing from their relationship. There's a disturbing emotional distance between them, and it is this distance, and their confusion about it, that causes the Stevenses to seek the help of a marriage counselor.

Donna is the one to make the initial contact with the counselor, and although I've heard the same words hundreds of times before, they never cease to move me. "We need help," Donna says. "I need more time to be alone with Nick, just the two of us. We never do anything together any more. We never talk. Not really."

With a little encouragement, she goes on to say: "We're so typical. Everyone thinks we're happy, the ideal couple, because we never fight. I mean, it isn't as if Nick weren't a nice guy or anything. He's given me a lot. I don't mean to sound ungrateful, but. . . ." Her voice trails off. As she grasps for words to describe her dilemma, it becomes clear that what puzzles her the most is the fact that she doesn't fit the usual description of the person who comes to a marriage counselor, nor can she find any rational explanation for not being happy with her life.

Donna explains that from a material point of view, she can hardly deny she has the best of everything. Furthermore, she has two beautiful children. The family has an adequate income—though who wouldn't like to have just a little more? Her husband doesn't beat her. He is not an alcoholic. He doesn't gamble. And as far as she knows, he has never had an affair with another woman. When she thinks about all these things, she feels ashamed for complaining. And that makes her feel even worse. She fears that she is a total neurotic, or at least well on her way to becoming one.

I assure Donna that she is not neurotic, nor are her complaints unfounded. I tell her and Nick that there are real solutions to the problems they are having. The way out for them, and for thousands of other couples in similar circumstances, is not through the divorce courts but through opening up the doors of their relationship. I tell them these doors could be thrown open by exploring a concept that I call the "marriage fantasy."

You're Fine — But Let's Take a Look at That Fantasy

The concept of fantasy, as I use it here, is not the same one we use when we describe a children's classic such as *Cinderella* or *Snow White*, or when we daydream about a special vacation we'd like to take or a fancy car that would be nice to own. Rather, the marriage fantasy has to do with the myriad of ideas about marriage that each of us collects from the day we are old enough to recognize that there *is* such a thing. It is, if you will, an inner vision that each of us feels is an essential part of our personal makeup. Indeed, the marriage fantasy does play a major part in making you who you are.

Each person learns about marriage through the culture in which he or she lives and, more directly, through observing his or her own parents. Without thinking about it, we have incorporated these teachings into our own way of thinking and feeling. One's total concept of marriage really does become a part of one's being.

The process of fantasizing is absolutely essential to life, inasmuch as the fantasy (as I use the term here) provides us with an internal guidance system for giving direction to our lives. However, we should all be alert to the fact that marriage is the most complicated relationship in the world, and most of the marriage fantasies that our culture offers just don't go far enough. Often a marriage fantasy works well for the first couple of years, but it then becomes a source of conflict and discontent as the years go by and different responsibilities confront the couple.

I have seen literally hundreds of couples discover the true power of their feelings for each other, feelings that endure past the marriage fantasy that brought them together in the first place. In a short time, for example, Nick and Donna learned that they had feelings for each other that endured beyond the marriage fantasy. They also learned that, ironically, the marriage fantasy had almost blinded them to the larger and more important part of their relationship.

If a couple is to enjoy fully the rich possibilities of marriage, both partners need to take a clear-sighted look at the thoughts and feelings that have gone into their own personal marriage fantasy. Just as though you were taking an inventory, you can examine your marriage fantasy to discover what *is* working well for you— most couples are amazed to find how much they do have working in their favor when they *really* look—and learn new skills that will add a whole new dimension to the relationships they have with their mates.

As one husband explained, it is almost as though the marriage fantasy takes on a life of its own, dictating our moves and the choices we make in relationship to our mate. Furthermore, we become free of the marriage fantasy when we look at it squarely and learn to see it for both its shortcomings and its merits. After that, perhaps it can be expanded and improved to make marriage the exciting and fulfilling experience it should be. Just as we may start out with a small house and add rooms, or move to a larger house as the family expands, so it becomes necessary to expand the marriage fantasy itself, or even leave it behind for a better one, as the relationship between husband and wife grows beyond the scope of their original vision.

How a Marriage Fantasy Is Built

Let's go back, for a moment, to Nick and Donna Stevens. What happened to them is similar to what happens to thousands of couples every year. They played out their marriage fantasies to the letter, but finally discovered that they could not make those fantasies become realities, no matter how hard they tried. In order to discover why this happens, let's take a look at how marriage fantasies develop. How is marriage taught in our culture and from what sources do we learn?

One major source of marriage information is our own family of origin, our parents. How did Mom and Dad get along? How did they handle conflicts, express feelings? How did they make their marriage what it is or what it was? Every day, from birth until we set out on our own, our parents are models for us, contributing to the construction of our own marriage fantasies, fantasies that will eventually guide our actions in our own marriages. Rarely do our parents teach us in any direct way, although most of us can remember favorite sayings by a family member. I often recall my own grandmother's observation that "marriage is a give-and-take situation."

One problem many people have with learning from their parents' marriage is that the marriage may have been a poor one. The parents may have had destructive fights or the children may have had incomplete pictures of their parents' relationship because the parents communicated their feelings for each other only behind closed doors. Even their affection for each other may have been expressed guardedly. When children fail to find satisfying models in their parents' relationship, they may seek models in society— often in movies or television shows. One problem with society's fantasy of marriage is that it is stereotypically rigid and not very responsive to change. People who act out this model of marriage take on a set of expectations that are destined to lead them to frustration and disappointment.

Another thing that can occur when people grow up with unsatisfying parental models of marriage is that they make an effort to compensate for the poor modeling by developing a concept of marriage that is the extreme opposite of what they witnessed as children. If the parents were always fighting and yelling at each other, their children may decide that when they get married, they won't fight and yell no matter what. They make a rule that any conflicts with their partner will be avoided at all costs. This concept of marriage may actually result in a less satisfying relationship than even their bickering parents had. The young couple has gone from one extreme to another, rather than seeking a middle ground where they could have a workable, realistic model for their marital relationship.

Even when our parents' marriage seemed "okay," this may have meant no more than the fact that they "got along" and stayed together to the "bitter end." Although this kind of stoic perseverance may have been a good model at one time, it is an outdated model. Men and women demand deeper personal satisfaction in their lives today.

An important source of ideas for building our marriage fantasies is the media, particularly television. With the advent of television in the 1950s, television programs have portrayed Hollywood's notion of what family and marriage is supposed to be. I can still remember how avidly I watched shows like "Ozzie and Harriet," "Father Knows Best," and "The Donna Reed Show." Everything I saw went into my memory banks, building my marriage fantasy. At the time, I wasn't aware of the *lessons* I was learning from watching these programs. My experience is probably shared by most people growing up in the 1950s—and the process is still going on for our own children. Most television shows of that era portrayed stereotypical and traditional views of how husbands and wives should relate to each other. Usually the woman stayed at home, taking care of the children. The man went off to work, but even during his absence maintained his position as "head of the household." Admittedly, there have been some changes in television programming since that time, but for the most part television continues to perpetuate traditional roles in marriage—most of which provide very inadequate models.

Most people are not well prepared for marriage. And yet we all believe we should somehow know exactly what we need to know to be a good wife or husband, a good mother or father. Society—and that certainly includes the media—falls far short of meeting the needs of couples in today's world. The myth is that if you "love each other enough," the marriage will work out fine. But this doesn't seem to be the case for most couples. It takes a great deal more than just being in love with your spouse to make a marriage work. It takes understanding and knowledge of how to solve problems, express anger, and still relate intimately. These are skills we never learned in school.

A New View of Domestic Crisis

Many people ask why the institution of marriage is in crisis now. What is causing the apparent breakdown of so many marriages? The fact that this institution is in crisis is not necessarily bad. A crisis is sometimes the catalyst required to bring about positive change. It is my observation that out of today's crises is evolving a new set of human skills that will eventually help married people meet the difficult challenges of modern society.

A major pressure on today's nuclear family has been inflation in the world's economy. Anyone trying to support a family knows only too well what I'm talking about. Every week the cost of food at the supermarket rises. Every time you buy your child a new pair of shoes, the price has taken a hike. Gasoline prices are sky-rocketing . . . and the list goes on. Inflation was once just a problem of juggling the family budget a little to meet the demands, but it's gone much farther than that.

Inflation has forced more and more women into the work force. Some, of course, go to work out of choice—that is, to satisfy personal needs not met by traditional roles. But many who want to stay at home can't do so because the second salaries they can earn are needed to maintain their families' living standard. This creates new pressures on the marriage because the wife working full time outside the home is not covered by the traditional marriage fantasy most of us learned. When she works full time at a job outside her home, the woman no longer has the time or energy to devote to being a wife and a mother. She is literally being expected to hold down two full-time jobs. The pressure is too much for any one person, and the stress she is under takes its toll.

There are no clearcut social roles or patterns to tell a woman how to be a working mother. If her own mother worked, she may have resented that her mother was gone so much, and she may have decided that when she had children, she would stay at home with them until they reached a certain age. But with the current inflation rate, that decision must often be sacrificed. In either case—whether she did not have a model or whether she has to make a sacrifice—the woman is set up for a great deal of frustration, tension, and anxiety.

The man, too, may experience problems because of the changing roles of the woman. He has learned that the man should be the "breadwinner" in the family. His wife should not have to work, but should be able to stay home and take care of the domestic responsibilities. Regardless of why his wife goes to work—be it out of choice or to meet the financial needs of the family—the man described here will not have his expectations fulfilled. He may not have the vaguest idea of how to relate to this new arrangement, and it is not unusual for men in this situation to feel emotionally threatened and to become defensive around the issue of their wives working. On the surface, the man may support the idea of his wife working and sharing the financial responsibilities, but he still expects his wife to take care of most of the domestic responsibilities. Of course, that's not a reasonable demand, but his expectations sprout from an emotional rather than an intellectual source within him. Inflation demands that adjustments be made in the basic structure of the American nuclear family, but lack of knowledge regarding these new demands upon the family, in combination with a rather human tendency to resist change, can cause a marital crisis to boil to the surface.

Women's Lib: New Freedoms or New Problems?

Another major factor that contributes to crises in many marriages is the development of the Women's Liberation Movement. Even women who don't identify themselves as feminists are questioning and, in many cases, no longer feel satisfied with "doing" things the way mother did." This new consciousness for women has spread through all levels of society. Not all people agree with what the leaders of the women's movement advocate, but whether they agree or disagree is not the issue I'm concerned with here. Regardless of one's political convictions, the reality we must face is that there are now viable alternatives to the traditional wife/ mother role for women. For the woman who experiences frustration in more traditional lifestyles, recognizing these alternatives is like finding a way out of a dark tunnel. The alternatives that the women's movement has created offer hope to the housewife and gain a following for the movement among women who were once alienated by the "bra burning image." Suddenly many women see it as a source of knowledge, a way to learn new skills to meet their needs.

But the alternatives offered require change, and with the prospect of change comes crisis. A woman is thrown into a state of conflict between what she *should* do and what she *wants* to do. This conflict is threatening to her husband who may—consciously or unconsciously—want a wife "just like mom." When the feeling of tension within the wife combines with pressure from her husband, conflict and instability within the family is inevitable. That conflict may well lead to positive change, but the process of getting to that point may require great patience and inner strength from everyone.

Pioneers in the Marriage Wilderness

With inflation and the women's movement upsetting the traditional marriage fantasy, most couples find themselves in crisis. Having been programmed with a highly unrealistic model of marriage, these people cannot help but feel a great amount of frustration and disappointment. They have all these emotions, but they have no place to go, no model, no new program to guide their decisions. Many choose to leave their present marriages and go out to try the whole thing all over again with someone else. It might be better the second time around, they tell themselves. All too often it's not.

What the young couple today must face is that there are no

adequate guidelines to define their roles as "good husbands" and "good wives." They are on their own, and like it or not, they must blaze their own trails and develop their own maps for this new territory. In time, these pioneers will bring mature change and stability to the institution of marriage—but those changes will demand as much from the young man and woman of today as the Wild West once demanded of our ancestors.

Trying Harder Can Deepen the Hurt

Some believe that with the easy accessibility of divorce, many couples don't try hard enough to make their marriages work. In my experience as a marriage counselor, this doesn't seem to be the case. On the contrary, couples generally do not give up easily, especially when they have invested several years together. Our typical couple, Nick and Donna, gives us an insight here. They have two nice children, a large amount of property, and they really don't hate each other in spite of their tensions. They do the opposite of quitting. They try even harder to play out the husband/wife roles that they learned as children, for they don't know what else to do. Sometimes I think all the couples I see share this common motto: "If you have a problem, work harder at it and that problem will be overcome." This is a variation of the Protestant Ethic. There seems to be a belief that there must be a way to achieve the standards of the traditional marriage fantasy they hold in their minds: "Somehow, we'll find it. We are just not trying hard enough." Struggling under this self-imposed pressure, the people in these relationships begin to feel inadequate. They get angry with themselves and angry with their partners for failing to make the marriage what it *should* be or what they had *hoped* it would be.

Despite the anger and hurt, and despite the tradition-bound remedies that couples try to apply to their marriage problems, the disappointment often remains and may even deepen. Time and again, men and women tell me that the harder they try to make their relationships work, the worse things seem to get. It's like spinning your car wheels in the sand. The faster you spin, the deeper you sink. However, the failure lies not in the effort, but in the method applied. It is as though today's couples are expecting to solve their problems by applying methods that only worked for problems that are now ancient history. For example: the woman of today isn't unwinding from her job at the end of the day when she rushes home to pick up the children at the babysitter, stop at the supermarket, and then iron her husband's shirts. No matter how well she does these things, she's not going to be relaxed and ready to enjoy her husband's company when he gets home. Nor is the husband going to make things better for himself by demanding that his wife rush home from work to clean house and have dinner ready when he arrives—regardless of how much he may want those things.

What I hope to show in the following chapters is why the marriage fantasy that most of us have learned won't work within the context of today's problems. But more important than this, I'll be suggesting some tried and true methods that meet the needs of today's couples. The first step toward solving our marriage problems is to become more aware of our marriage fantasies, of the roles that society has laid upon us, and of how we are supposed to go about fulfilling our own expectations of how marriage should be. Once two people have become aware of how they have been brought up or how they have been taught to think about marriage, they can begin to bring about constructive changes in themselves. Without this awareness, the couple is on automatic pilot set for a rendezvous with crisis. They just act out the roles of what a good wife and a good husband are supposed to be, blind to the fact that they are setting the stage for major problems.

My purpose here is not to describe what a "right" marriage is supposed to be or to present another set of rules for people to follow. It is to give couples the knowledge to free themselves from their marriage fantasies and to develop methods designed to meet the real needs of their own individual circumstances. The tools you will find here will take you to greater levels of intimacy with your mate while shrinking the dimensions of everyday problems. I have seen these tools work time and time again in my professional practice, bringing couples together with the least amount of struggle.

Be prepared to give up your notions about what "should" be; discover, instead, what works.

2. A Script for Bliss and Crisis

At this point, let us explore the traditional marriage fantasy as it has been played out by hundreds of couples. This scenario is a generalized pattern. Of course, in real life there may be infinite variations, differences that may vary according to cultural background, ethnic group, or economic status. For the record, the group from which I've derived these generalizations primarily consists of middle-class to upper middle-class white suburban families.

The Stage Is Set

Our scenario begins with two "players"—that is, two separate selves (see Figure 1) who are not romantically involved with one another. The word *self* in this context encompasses all the things that make up one's self-identity—career, hobbies, family background, friends, feelings, aspirations, and so forth. The self is ev-

Figure 1

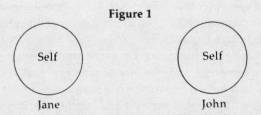

erything that you are or have a potential for becoming. Some people develop a sense of themselves before they get married, but many of us don't get a chance to explore who we are as individuals because we get married so young. It's hard to get a sense of yourself at twenty-one or twenty-two in a culture that prolongs adolescence. Many women get married before they've had the experience of being "out on their own." They go from being their fathers' daughters to being their husbands' wives without ever having a chance to explore and develop a strong sense of who they are and what's really important to them as individuals separate from their fathers' and husbands' opinions and values.

The same kind of developmental patterns can happen to men, too. Many men get married right after high school or college and immediately assume all the financial pressures and responsibilities of supporting a family. They never really have a chance to live as single adults, to explore what their options and interests might be apart from the pressures of meeting their families' needs.

The self is the person's basic foundation, the wellspring of his or her thoughts and feelings, and in this respect it becomes the foundation upon which a marriage is built. The stronger the sense of personal identity that people bring to their marriage, the stronger their relationship will be—and the less likely they will be to allow self-destructive patterns to develop.

When Two Become One

What happens when two selves meet and decide to get married? It matters very little whether these two individuals get married right out ot their parents' homes, whether they marry after having been single for a long time, or whether they live together for a couple of years before legally establishing themselves as married. The same process occurs in any case, a process that engages each party's marriage fantasies.

What happens is like data ("I'm a husband"; "I'm a wife") being fed into a computer, and this information eventually dictates the expectations and behavior of the two marriage partners. The computer tapes, if you will, contain the marriage fantasies, most of which have been programmed by society to tell the young couple what the good wife and the good husband should do.

When the tapes start rolling—that is, when the couple begins playing out the marriage fantasy—neither partner is very aware of it. This process is most clearly illustrated with the man and woman who have been living together for a year or two. Frequently, they resist the social pressure to get married, sensing the danger of falling into what they perceive as "the marriage trap."

For many couples who make this transition from living together to getting married, the computer tapes come into play so subtly they hardly notice. The first signs of change come when they stop relating to each other as individuals and start being *husband* and *wife*. The man starts trying to do all the things society taught him a husband needs to do, and he begins to expect his mate to do all the things society teaches him that a wife should do. And, of course, the same patterns occur for the woman as well. That's when the trouble starts, because the marriage fantasies obscure and in a very real way depersonalize the two partners. How often people have told me: "We were living together and things were going really well until we decided to get married. Since then things have not been the same. It was better before."

When a couple first gets married, they tend to give a lot of time and energy to each other. They are together a lot and their relationship is their first priority (see Figure 2). This period of time is often intense and romantic. The man and woman are very excited about being with each other. Frequently, because the relationship takes up so much time, they give less time to their own selves. A

Figure 2

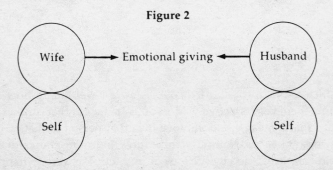

woman may leave school, move away from her friends, or quit working. The same thing happens to the man. He may decide he has less time for his single friends because "their heads aren't in the same place anymore." He may stop doing some of his challenging activities, for he is married now and therefore more "stable and mature" (see Figure 3).

Figure 3

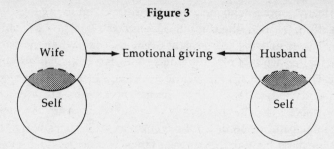

Another thing that occurs when two people get married is an increase in the number of conflicts. In any marriage, there are two different individuals, with two different family backgrounds, value systems, and different ways of doing even small things, so there are bound to be conflicts (see Figure 4). The problem with

Figure 4

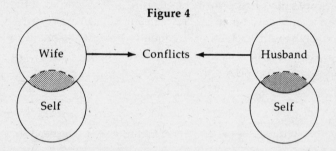

conflicts is that most married couples were never taught how to handle them very effectively. Most of us are taught that conflict is "bad," that it means we don't love the other person or that he or she doesn't love us. Naturally, this causes the young couple to be afraid and threatened by the idea of conflict: "We were so happy being married. We didn't want to start fighting with each other."

But conflict, and the fear of it, doesn't go away. It is virtually impossible to live with another person—*any* other person—without experiencing some conflict. Although the young husband and wife may exercise great self-control, there comes the day when they can no longer sweep their resentments "under the rug" or keep "selling out" to avoid disagreements. They have a fight—

and usually it's a big one. A fight, by my definition, is a conflict that results in a breakdown of communication, a breakdown that results because both individuals get caught up in the idea of "winning"—that is, each tries to prove that his or her position is the right and true way that should be adopted as the standard in the marriage. The fight may not split them up and end their marriage (even if one leaves for awhile), but their experience of this conflict may be so unpleasant and threatening that they don't want it to happen again. It's as if they decide to take all their resentments and lock them up behind a thick vault door. In most cases, this decision is made at an unconscious level, and once that door is closed, the husband and wife put increasing energy into maintaining the status quo, "trying to keep our marriage as happy as it was when we first got together" (see Figure 5). However, their efforts often lead them down a path toward boredom and a particular kind of loneliness.

Figure 5

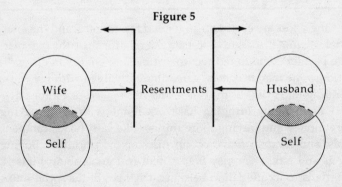

Self-Control Can Squelch Intimacy

It's difficult to be emotionally close or intimate with someone who has made you angry, even though you've closed the big door on the resentments you feel. The cost of closing the door on conflicts, for the sake of a few moments of calm, is the dulling of all feelings of intimacy and emotional closeness. An emotional vacuum begins to develop in the marriage. It isn't as if the two partners are not getting along with each other. They may look happy to outsiders, and they may even think of themselves as happy, but their behavior becomes more predictable. The intensity of feelings they had for each other when they first got together seems to have faded—and yet, they don't want to talk about this change, even if they are aware of the difference, which often they aren't (see Figure 6). It's hard to express warm, caring feelings for your mate if you feel you can't tell him when you're even a little bit annoyed.

Figure 6

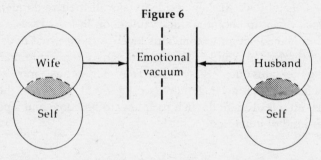

As the doors are closed on anger and resentment, and the emotional vacuum begins to dominate the relationship, the two marriage partners tend to redirect their time and energy in other directions. The man becomes increasingly involved with his work, spending more time at the office, and in some cases, either physically or mentally bringing his work home with him. Making more money and buying more things (like cars, boats, campers, pools, and houses) move up on his scale of priorities. Buying things and having money help a man feel good about himself. Materialistic accumulation becomes a symbol of his social status and an expression of his self-identity. When he isn't working or playing with the things he has bought, he gets involved in social or community groups. The important thing, he believes, is to keep busy, to be "doing something," for he has a hard time relaxing and doing nothing. He may argue that if he were to slow down and relax, he would not be "accomplishing anything." But more importantly, he might become more aware of what is missing in his marriage. And that would be too threatening and uncomfortable (see Figure 7).

Figure 7

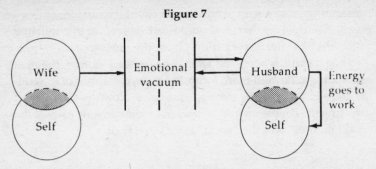

The woman in the marriage may also feel the emotional vacuum at this point in her marriage and, like her husband, may be unconsciously afraid to confront it. She may fill this vacuum in one of two ways. First, she may decide to follow the same path as her husband. Her main priority then becomes herself, primarily her career. With both partners working, this couple can do well financially and materially, but an emotional vacuum still exists between them. Soon this couple's relationship becomes more like that of roommates, with financial independence for both. And when no children are involved, this couple is unlikely to stay together for very long if their emotional needs continue to go unfulfilled.

The second way in which this woman can fill the emotional vacuum in her marriage is by having children. She has been told—and it is true—that having a child will fulfill some of her emotional needs, needs that are no longer being met in her relationship with her husband. I hasten to add that by no means is her need for an alternative source of emotional fulfillment the main reason for her decision to have a baby. It can be argued that the drives involved here can best be described as belonging to the "mysteries of life." It is perhaps an error to attempt to explain all the reasons a young couple decides to have a child, but sometimes they are extremely clear about it. It is common, for example, for a couple to tell me that they had children in order to "hold our marriage together," or to "improve our relationship with each other." It is no coincidence, I am convinced, that "unplanned" pregnancies occur so frequently about the time that couples are considering breaking up. And I cannot count the number of times people have told me that they would get divorced, or that splitting up would be easier, if they didn't have the kids.

When a child is born, the woman becomes a mother, the man becomes a father, and more computer tapes come into play, sending out signals from the marriage fantasies. Now the signals start directing the couple on how to play out their two new roles of the "good mother" and the "good father" (see Figure 8).

Figure 8

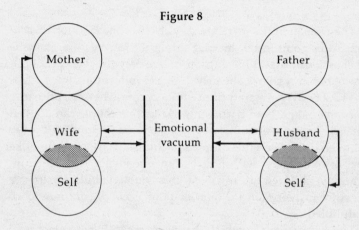

Being a "good mother" usually involves an outpour of the woman's time and energy. In fact, in the beginning, it's almost a twenty-four hour job of constant giving, with occasionally some relief from the father. So now we have a woman giving huge blocks of time and energy to her child, while giving somewhat less time to her husband. She still cooks for him, cleans his clothes, and generally takes care of him. And by the end of the day, there isn't much time for herself. Indeed, her self needs are sacrificed to the needs of her family. The woman may not be aware of what is happening to her, for she is just too busy giving to everyone else. But were she to do otherwise, she would run the risk of feeling guilty and selfish (see Figure 9), because her marriage fantasy says that a good wife and mother is supposed to sacrifice her self for the sake of her family.

Figure 9

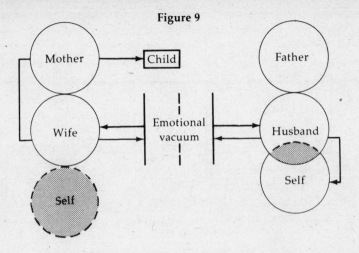

At this point, the woman puts both herself and her marriage in a precarious position. If she gives too little to herself, she will develop a great deal of emotional resentment. Not being aware of how self-denial eats at her, she will continue giving to others, while her resentment collects and builds. Soon her controlled resentments begin to surface in somewhat camouflaged ways: she may be less interested in sex, or become critical of other people, or feel vaguely depressed without being able to explain why. Her self-esteem drops. Though she may not be fully aware of it, she has started to resent her husband and children. Unfortunately, she can hardly admit these feelings, because her marriage fantasy tells her that having them is wrong.

The man can also become very involved in being a father, of course, and spend a great deal of his free time giving to his children. This pattern is very common in suburbia, where a couple's relationship often becomes centered around their children (see Figure 10). Child-related activities, such as PTA, Little League baseball, soccer games, and Boy Scouts and Girl Scouts, become common weekend or evening activities. Whenever this couple does something without their children, they tend to have other couples with them. Unconsciously, they avoid time alone together. Not that there's anything wrong with spending time with

Figure 10

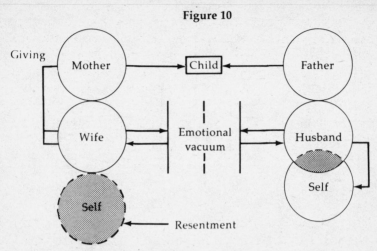

one's children or with other couples, but when such activities are used by a husband and wife to avoid intimacy, problems often develop. A question I ask couples is, "How often do you sit down alone, just the two of you, without the t.v. and with no children around, no diversions?" Usually the answer is that they don't do it very often because they don't have the time or they simply don't think about doing it.

The reason such a couple avoids being alone together is that by now, maybe six to seven years into their marriage, the conflicts and resentments that were never adequately resolved or expressed at the beginning of their marriage have come very close to the surface. When they are alone, they fear that after they've gotten through the superficial material in their conversation, the old conflicts and resentments will bubble forth. They were not able to handle these conflicts in the beginning when there were only a few. Now the number of conflicts has increased, and so has their emotional intensity. They become afraid that each conflict, no matter how small, may snowball and overcome them. As a result, the couple avoids any real intimacy and finds as many diversions as possible—diversions that usually have reasonable explanations and purposeful goals.

Even though this couple is clearly on shaky ground, they look fine to themselves and to their friends. And why not? They never seem to have any conflicts, they have so many friends, and they lead such an active social life. They also spend a lot of time with their kids. Of course, some things in their marriage relationship have become predictable and routine, like their sexual relationship, but they just write that off to the fact that they've been together for eight to nine years, and isn't it natural for people to lose interest in each other after so much time? As we shall soon see, sexual pleasure can actually increase with the years—if the couple learns how to evaluate and change their marriage fantasies.

The Crisis Begins

The stage has been set for the crisis in this couple's marriage. The crisis is started by two events. The first event usually involves the woman in the marriage. As her children become more involved in their own activities, such as school and playing with friends, less and less of her time and energy needs to be directed toward them. The woman begins to slow down and stops "chasing around like a chicken with its head cut off," as so many women have put it. With more time on her hands, she becomes increasingly aware of her own needs, and she starts getting in touch with what is missing in her relationship with her husband. With this new awareness, the woman tries to shift her interest back to her husband, making efforts to communicate more fully and spend more time with him. She starts to tear down the emotional wall she erected many years back. She no longer wishes to hold her feelings back, but letting them go isn't easy either. To some extent, habit prevents her from changing. But in addition, there is nothing in her marriage fantasy to guide her. She may try to delay this process and get involved in herself by going back to school or getting a job. This is a good start towards taking care of herself, and it helps raise her self-esteem. However, her efforts don't create greater intimacy or improve communications with her husband. It may upset her husband that his wife is changing the status quo. The change in her behavior may even cause him enough discomfort to force him to open his own emotional barriers (see Figure 11).

When the woman tries to communicate with her husband, she

Figure 11

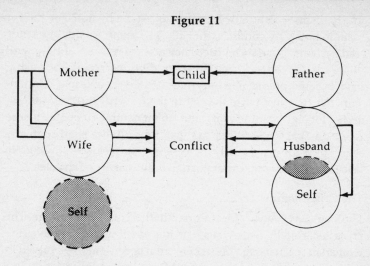

may have a hard time reaching him, for at this time in his life, he may be too involved in his work or his hobbies. All he wants is peace. He just can't understand why she isn't happy. After all, he has "busted his butt" working to buy all those things—the pool, the nice house in the suburbs, everything needed to complete the American Dream—and she still isn't happy. He has been trying to do all the right things, everything dictated by his marriage fantasy, everything that a good husband should do, and he can't help but feel resentful and defensive. He now has a hard time listening to his wife. It's as if they were living in two different worlds. And though each may blame the other, the truth of the matter is: neither of them is to blame. They have both done the best they know how. They gave their all, as the saying goes. The marriage fantasy is now the crisis.

What Happens After the Door Is Opened?

As husband and wife begin to communicate their dissatisfactions and resentments, they become increasingly more hurt and frustrated. When they start to handle one problem, twenty-five more seem to come up, and they soon feel overwhelmed. They didn't have the communication skills in the beginning to deal with the intense emotions of conflict, and they have difficulty developing these skills in the midst of a crisis in their relationship. At this stage, the couple's relationship may worsen, and they either separate or seek out counseling (see Figure 12).

Figure 12

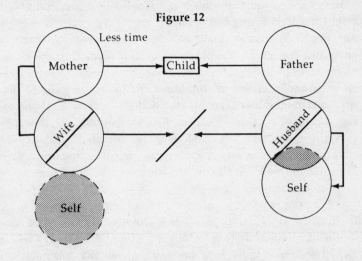

Another way this particular crisis in marriage is acted out is by one partner having an extramarital affair and the other partner learning about it. At this stage in the couple's marriage, they are both hungry for intimacy, romance, and excitement. If someone would pay attention to their romantic needs, they would be delighted. So if the right situation comes up, the man or the woman may become involved with another person. It's not as if he or she goes out looking for this involvement, though that's often the popular conception. Most people say that "it just seems to happen." And the affair is discovered in much the same unconscious manner. The partner involved in the affair "accidentally" leaves some clue around for his or her mate to find. The "other person" in the extramarital relationship is often someone the couple has known socially or someone at work. Usually this person is convenient, and some type of relationship has been already established. This is quite the opposite of the picture of the "one night stand," so often popularized in movies.

The extramarital relationship is an effort to get everything that the person is missing in her or his marriage on an intimate level.

The affair is exciting, romantic, full of passion, and doesn't have ten years of stored-up resentment to get in the way. On the other hand, it lacks the emotional security of a marriage.

For most couples, the affair is not as selfishly motivated as one might think. Working with couples who have gone through it, one quickly learns that it is often an unconscious effort to create a crisis and change the couple's marriage. It tends to make either one partner or both examine what they have and, in many cases, make powerful efforts to communicate honestly, maybe for the first time in their marriage. This is a period of intense soul-searching, a time to see if they really do love each other. The affair may also trigger a breakup. It provides a clear-cut issue. Perhaps they couldn't take responsibility for the breakup in a more direct way. They had to create something, and the extramarital affair seems to provide an adequate excuse.

One of the byproducts of separation or divorce, expecially for the woman in the relationship, is that when her role of being a mother declines and she is no longer a wife, she is left only with a buried self (see Figure 13). She is like a seed that has been left

Figure 13

dormant and needs some nurturing before it will grow and become a beautiful flower. I see many women like this—women who don't know what to do with their lives. It's exciting and frightening for them to embark on the road to finding out what they are all about. Many go back to college and enter women's re-entry programs, or they seek employment so they can better support themselves and help build their self-esteem.

The man, on the other hand, may not reach his marriage fantasy crisis—or "male menopause," as some call it—until he loses interest in the primary ways in which he made himself feel good, mainly making money and buying things. There is no definite age when this happens, but it seems to occur about the time he reaches the top of the corporate ladder or realizes that he won't be able to make any more money than he presently does. As one man told me, "What else is there to do after I get my Mark IV Continental and my big house on the hill?" He starts to question what life is all about, and he starts to change his values, to put less importance on material things, to seek more from his personal life.

If we allow ourselves to play out the marriage fantasy programmed by our culture, our marriage cannot help but end in crisis. The challenge facing couples today is how to keep all their roles—mother-father, wife-husband, and self—in balance. Having a child certainly is a major responsibility. Being married is a responsibility, too. But don't forget your responsibility to your self. When the self in both marriage partners is not nurtured, the ability to perform the other two roles (wife-mother, husband-father) will be dramatically weakened. In some situations, especially among women, a backlash occurs. She rebels or reacts from so much self-denial. She leaves marriage behind to go out and "do her own thing." She goes from one extreme to another, denying her need for intimacy. This doesn't work either, because she still has responsibilities, and becoming totally self-oriented doesn't make those responsibilities go away.

What is the answer? Is the institution of marriage, like the dinosaur, on its way to becoming extinct? I'd like to voice a responding cheer in support of marriage. But let there be no illusions about it, couples of today must blaze new trails, must pioneer a new set of values to create marriage fantasies that will really answer their needs.

3. *The Good-Wife Fantasy*

The "good wife" is the role cast for the woman in the marriage fantasy. Most of this role has been taught to the woman, usually in indirect ways, starting from the day she was born. By the time she is old enough to marry, she has learned her lessons so well that she is not even aware the fantasy came from sources outside herself. The marriage fantasy is now working from within, guiding her courtship and marriage decisions.

What kinds of rules dictate her marriage role, and how do they affect her? That's what this chapter is about. We'll first explore the main elements of the "good wife" role and then examine some of the things that happen when a woman attempts to play out this role.

1. The good wife should not think about herself; she should not be selfish.

The good wife should not place much importance on self-development. The idea of developing any career or marketable skill is to be discouraged. Self-development is okay only so long as it is oriented toward attracting her husband or keeping him attracted to her. She must believe that she needs the man to make her feel complete. To avoid guilt about her own selfishness, the woman must give selflessly to her husband. The underlying principle of this role is that if your husband is happy, then you most certainly will be happy, too.

2. The good wife should try to please her husband.

It is the wife's responsibility to make sure that her husband is happy and well cared for at all times. Not that there is anything wrong with wanting to please someone you love (there isn't), but it is difficult, if not impossible, to be responsible for another person's happiness. This impossible demand is made even more difficult because her concern for her husband's happiness must take priority over her concern for her own happiness. This part of her role manifests in numerous ways, but one way in which it manifests and causes much conflict in marriage is by requiring that the "good wife" be at home whenever her husband is there, regardless of what her needs might be. This seemingly simple demand has the effect of reminding the woman that she is subservient to her husband.

3. *The good wife should not do anything that would threaten her husband.*

This rule fits right into the idea of the wife's self-denial. After all, if she were to improve herself, she might threaten her husband. So she certainly shouldn't get a better job than he has or make more money than he does, nor should she show that she is more knowledgeable or influential than her husband in any area of life. She should never disagree with her husband in public nor let anyone know that she and her husband are not totally happy. She should also try to do all the same activities as her husband—golfing, tennis, skiing, etc.—but she should not do any of them better than he does. Her job is to build the feeling and impression of togetherness and harmony in their marriage.

4. *The good wife should not take responsibility for what she wants in her marriage.*

It is her husband's job, not hers, to decide what's important in the marriage. This rule is a major one for most women in our culture. Women who break this rule by making demands often experience a great deal of fear and guilt. The wife who starts taking responsibility for family decisions and asking for what she wants from her husband runs the risk of becoming a nag, or worse, what is popularly known as a "bitch." Why should she have to tell her husband what she wants anyway? If he's as good a husband as she is a wife and if he really loves her, he will know what she wants—or so the marriage fantasy goes.

5. *The good wife should take care of all the domestic responsibilities: the cooking, cleaning, washing, and shopping.*

These activities are "women's work," according to the traditional marriage fantasy. The good wife should never even question the fact that the household chores are her territory. That's what her mother did for her father, and that's what they taught her in homemaking class in high school, and that is what she has seen on television and in movies. This part of the marriage fantasy continues to apply even when the woman has a full-time job outside the house.

6. *The good wife should be her husband's emotional support.*
She is not only responsible for pleasing her husband, but she is responsible for taking care of his emotional needs. Many a husband denies that he needs his wife's emotional support—that is, until she threatens to leave him or starts divorce proceedings. She is responsible for making sure his ego and self-image are in good shape, which relates to that other rule about not threatening his ego. The great business or professional man can run his "big business machine" very well until his emotional supply line is cut, when his wife stops giving to him emotionally. This rule is reflected in the old saying, "Behind every successful man is a good wife."

Now that we have looked at some of the rules for being a good wife in our culture, I want to look at what happens to a woman's emotional life when she tries to live her life by these rules. Of course, as we go over these points, the reader should recognize that we are describing general patterns and that there are as many variations on them as there are people. Even so, it will prove helpful to begin with these patterns, patterns which I've found repeated many times over among the married couples with whom I've worked.

The Woman's Rewards for Being a Good Wife

The emotional consequences of living out the role of the good wife in today's world are numerous and nearly impossible to escape. On the basis of my experiences with hundreds of couples, I have no reservations at all about saying that women who try to conform to this role have extremely difficult marriages. While the program may look good from the outside, the truth is that it is doomed to failure. The central emotional hazard is that the wife must put her husband's and her children's needs above her own. A person whose needs for self-fulfillment are being thwarted will normally feel discomfort, and often it takes the form of anger, anxiety, and low self-esteem. Though a woman who is trying to be a good wife may deny that this is the case, the discomfort is most obvious among women who got a taste of self-fulfillment in college or a job and then shut down that process to become good wives. At first, such a woman may find it feels good to give everything up to get married. She gives up her name, says good-bye to old lovers and friends, and closes savings and checking accounts, often putting everything she owns into her husband's name. Unless she and her husband make a special effort to guarantee her financial rights, the woman completely loses any credit rating she may have had when she was single. And yet, many a woman reports that, in the beginning, nothing felt better than to "put myself in my husband's hands."

No wonder the good wife tends to experience a deep sense of confusion when the marriage fantasy starts to break down. Suddenly, everything she believed to be true is proving to be untrue in her life. Suddenly, she's caught, not able to change her role because, first, she is usually unaware of alternatives and, second, her husband, also unaware of what else to do, is not supportive of change. Being stuck is uncomfortable, and so resentment begins to grow. And although the wife's resentment may only be a spark, that spark, more often than not, ignites a raging flame that threatens to engulf both marriage partners.

The resentment usually doesn't come directly to the surface, but is held in by the person who feels it. In recent years, the term *stuffing* has been applied to this process of burying or holding in feelings of anger, resentment, frustration, and hurt. It is a very graphic term and useful in our discussion here.

The most common reaction to the stuffing process is depression. The depression may be expressed in different degrees, from just feeling low on energy to literally not wanting to get out of bed in the morning. The stuffing process often begins as a conscious decision, but soon it becomes something done without thinking.

In playing out the role of the good wife, the woman is usually unable to get angry and express her true feelings of resentment. This is not to say that she doesn't ever get mad, but when she does, it usually comes across as an "irrational outburst" or in the form of tears, which are neither effective nor accurate ways of communicating. Furthermore, she usually feels guilty about these expressions later on and may even apologize, thus diffusing any movement toward getting her grievances heard. Not having an effective means of expressing her anger, the good wife finds herself caught up in a vicious circle of stuffing her feelings until she can't stand it any longer, at which time she blows up, then apologizes or makes excuses for the blow up and starts stuffing again, repeating the fruitless cycle again and again.

One reason the good wife stuffs her feelings is because she is afraid she will be viewed as a "bitch" or a nag. She has learned that women are awarded such titles whenever they express anger or resentment. In the face of this threat, she may come to the conclusion that her only option is to avoid expressing herself, to repress or hide her feelings. For example, if the woman were to tell her husband that it bothers her when he leaves his clothes on the floor, they might fight about that issue. This would upset their fantasy of being "a happy couple." And since she knows she is supposed to make her husband happy, she tells herself that "it's not that big of a deal" and continues to pick up after her husband instead of asking him to take that responsibility himself. The trouble is that while her husband is not taking responsibility for picking up after himself, the wife is not taking responsibility for communicating her feelings.

The single most difficult part of the good-wife marriage fantasy is the notion that she should keep her husband happy. This part of the fantasy, more than anything else, inhibits the woman in expressing her true feelings, feelings which, if the woman is normal, may upset or threaten the man. In her efforts to fulfill the dictates of her marriage fantasy, she hides her feelings, in a way protecting her husband from the discomfort he might experience if she were more honest. The result, for her, is usually a form of depression she can't explain.

Depression is one major source of emotional discomfort women experience in trying to fulfill their role as good wives, but there are others. A woman may express a sense of constant irritation with the world around her. She is often labeled a "nag" or a "bitch" or "uptight." However, she is not consciously choosing this style of expression. Like the woman who is depressed, she is reflecting the resentment, anger, frustration, and hurt she feels. Often, it seems to her and to everyone around her that nothing can make her happy. And, the fact is that nothing will until she takes it upon herself to liberate herself from the good-wife marriage fantasy. Like the woman who is depressed, this woman knows she is resentful and angry, but she is not aware of the connection between the difficulty she has communicating her needs, the fantasy that dictates her decisions, and her unhappiness. To her, it just feels as though the world is presenting her with a never-ending list of aggravations.

Unlike the depressive type, the nagging or negative woman doesn't hold in her feelings. Instead, she "dumps" them on her husband, blames and attacks him verbally. Her criticisms focus on the "little things"—for example, his forgetting to call when he is going to be late or his making a relatively minor decision without considering her opinion. Although these can be real issues, her responses to them are often out of proportion to their importance. What's important for this woman to realize is that her complaints often act as a smoke screen, preventing her from seeing the more personal underlying problem—the painful lack of self-fulfillment caused by the untenable dictates of her marriage fantasy.

Many women who are trying to conform to the good-wife fantasy, with its denial of self-development, attempt to desensitize themselves to resentment and pain through overeating, alcohol, and even drugs. All these can help reduce some of the discomforts of frustration, anger, hurt, and resentment, but they do nothing whatsoever to correct their causes. The causes of the woman's emotional discomfort continue, and so does her discomfort and her need to desensitize herself. If this pattern is prolonged over many years, the woman's already limited inner resources are taxed further, and she breaks down emotionally, perhaps with some physical damage to her body.

I can hear some of you saying, "But not all women who play the traditional good-wife fantasy are unhappy." Most of us know women who say that they are happy being good wives, that they feel good about themselves. But before we set these people up as models of success, let us remember that being happy with the good-wife role is one of the central features of that fantasy. I'm not saying it's impossible to be happy being a wife, but there is no doubt in my mind that it is impossible to be happy trying to conform to the good-wife fantasy we've been examining here. We should recognize that people do gain a certain amount of satisfaction from proving they can do something that society and their parents have been trying to teach them for a number of years— and being able to follow the plan for the good wife is no exception. If a woman has been well prepared, she may even take pride in her ability to hide her resentment. But be assured that in spite of her claims to the contrary, it is a rare woman who doesn't feel uncomfortable playing the role of the good wife that society, her parents, and her peers have spelled out for her.

Outside Influences Support Good-Wife Fantasies

The woman has many pressures on her to be a good wife, and these pressures can be emotionally painful in themselves. Often there is parental pressure to be a good wife, and this pressure is increased when a woman is also still trying to win her father's or mother's acceptance. It is not unusual, by any means, for parents to express their wishes that their daughter have a happy marriage, a nice house, a loyal and happy husband, and beautiful children. Parents don't have to express these expectations directly. More often than not, they express their expectations through stories about this person and her "wonderful husband," or the "lovely grandchildren" the woman next door has. But whether her parents communicate their expectations directly or indirectly, the daughter who has been taught the good-wife fantasy will feel pressure to satisfy them. If it is still important to her that she win her parents' acceptance, fulfilling her parents' expectations may take priority over fulfilling her own needs for self-development outside the marriage fantasy.

In addition to a woman's parents, her husband also puts pressure on her to be a good wife. His expectations, we must remember, come from the same sources that teach the woman what she should do to be a good wife. Both husband and wife have developed expectations about what a woman must do in a marriage by watching their parents and listening to society's values. It is quite understandable that the good wife would want to please both her husband and parents, but the price of self-denial, as we've already learned, can be terribly destructive.

Physical Beauty and Self-Esteem

All of us have mental images of our physical attractiveness and these images are shaded as much by our general feelings about ourselves as by our actual physical attributes. Thus, an extremely beautiful woman might have an image of herself as ugly, if her self-esteem is low, while an ordinary or even physically ugly woman might have a self-image of herself as beautiful. A person's self-perceptions of her body come from a great many, rather complex sources, but the good-wife fantasy frequently contributes to a negative self-image. In her efforts to please her husband, a woman often tries to live up to his fantasies of ultimate female beauty, and usually these fantasies are highly unrealistic, not to be achieved by any human. If she realizes that she can't change to meet these expectations, the woman may become embarrassed or ashamed of her body. She may keep the lights off in the bedroom, and if her husband, or someone else, tells her she is beautiful, she may have a difficult time enjoying the compliment. Regardless of how attractive others find her, the woman with a negative self-image will find something wrong: too fat, too skinny, too big, too small. Whatever she is, she feels it's not good enough, even though she may have been told she is beautiful or knows she should learn to accent her own unique beauty. Unable to accept herself physically, she may feel threatened by other women and always feel in competition with them. The woman who cannot accept herself physically also cannot accept the idea that her husband likes her just the way she is. As a result, she may believe her husband is more attracted to other women than he is to her.

The Good Wife's Dependency on Her Husband

The woman entangled in the good-wife marriage fantasy ordinarily develops a strong feeling of dependency on her husband.

The amount of dependency seems to increase in proportion to the length of time the role is played. By accepting the role and giving up responsibility for communicating her feelings and making decisions, a woman may become as dependent on her husband as a child on her father. Because her husband does certain things for her, such as fixing the car, paying the bills, and keeping the house in good repair, the woman never gets the opportunity to learn about these things. And as a result of her lack of experience, she often comes to believe that such tasks are outside her capacities and she needs her husband to do these "masculine" jobs. Often, because she feels helpless and dependent on him, she also feels resentful, and she expresses her resentment by nagging him about the things that he has failed to do or has done in a way she doesn't like. Of course, there is nothing inherently wrong in a wife asking her husband to fix the car, but there is a problem when she begins to feel this is the only way it can get done. Such experiences may give her the impression that she has a void which only her husband can fill.

The fear that she cannot do the things her husband does for her keeps many women afraid to abandon their good-wife fantasies. When faced with the prospect of learning how to do the things classified as masculine duties in her marriage fantasy, she confronts a second fear—the fear that if she becomes too independent, her independence might threaten or anger her husband and he might leave her. It may seem that the easiest thing for her to do is to protect the status quo and not rock the boat.

A woman with low self-esteem, one who views herself as inadequate, unattractive, or incapable of learning, easily falls into dependency patterns that perpetuate these feelings. Unfortunately, the good-wife fantasy tends to maintain a woman's low self-esteem. Time and again, women in counseling are asked why they stay with husbands who they admit treat them badly. The most common answer is, "I love him." When probed further or asked *why* they love their husband, most women reply that he is a "good provider" or a "good father." But they don't say what they feel about him as a person. I believe that women in this situation are not so much in love with the person to whom they are married as they are in love with what he stands for: financial security and protection from the fear of being alone in the world.

Today's society tends to put value on a person according to the marketable skills that he or she possesses. Being a housewife is highly valuable within the context of a nuclear family, but it doesn't pay much outside that context. It doesn't provide a woman with skills valued in the marketplace. No matter how much a woman prides herself on her capacities as a housewife, she knows that her skills won't help her establish financial autonomy in the same way that being a lawyer or an auto mechanic might. This realization adds to her sense of being dependent on a husband.

It can be seen that the consequences of playing out the role of the good wife may include depression, low self-esteem, and varying degrees of dependency. All of these emotional factors flow together, overlapping into a complex web within the good wife's mind. The net result, time and again, is anger, fear, and hurt. All of these grow from the fertile mud of unexpressed emotion.

Almost all the women I see in counseling deny, in a perfectly honest way, that they feel any anger. This should be emphasized, first, because it happens so often and, second, because I am certain that these women really believe they are not angry. I can say this because I have watched women in counseling discover their own anger as they learn to liberate themselves from their marriage fantasies. The reason women don't feel their own anger is that they have never been allowed to express that feeling: anger is not "womanly." A woman is taught to be a "good girl," which means, in essence, that she is taught to stuff her anger and smile. Eventually, she becomes anesthetized to the feeling. She becomes depressed perhaps, controlled and quiet, bored with the apparent limits of her life. But angry? Never.

Feelings are real. They must be expressed in ways that somehow satisfy the person who experiences them. In the case of unexpressed anger, the feelings that are turned inward cause increasingly more pain, de-energizing that person and contaminating everything he or she does. Breaking this circle of disillusionment and discomfort begins with the awareness of the good-wife component of the marriage fantasy.

4. The Good-Husband Fantasy

Just as there is a good-wife component in the traditional marriage fantasy, so there is a good-husband role. Like his wife, the man learns his part in the fantasy by observing his parents and through models supported by society. Not as much has been written about being a good husband as has been written about being a good wife. The women's movement has been responsible for examining the woman's role, disseminating information about it, and offering alternatives. But little has been done about men in this regard. Indeed, the popular illusion is that the husband is content with his role and requires no liberation or information about alternatives. Nothing could be further from the truth. The man is as frustrated in his role as a good husband as the woman is frustrated in her role as a good wife. Like his wife, the man is on automatic pilot much of the time, hardly aware of the choices he is making as a husband. Let's take a close look at the husband's part in the marriage fantasy and explore some of the rules that guide his behavior.

1. The good husband should not appear vulnerable or weak.
This rule applies not only to the good husband, but to men in general. He should never appear weak or emotional. He is the *strong* one of the two sexes. As the husband, he must be a "stable rock" so that his wife can feel safe and secure.

2. The good husband should keep his work and his home life separate.
The good husband should not "bother" his wife with all the problems he confronts in his work, since she has enough of her own problems at home. Besides, the man must realize that his problems may cause her to worry about their economic future, and it is his duty as a good husband to protect her from such worries. When he is at home he should enjoy his time with his family and forget the problems of the day. Besides, the marriage fantasy teaches the man

to believe that even if he tried to discuss his work problems with his wife, she probably wouldn't understand them. At best, she would probably find them boring.

3. *The good husband should not be dependent on anyone, including his wife.*

The good husband should be self-reliant, taking care of himself in all facets of life. He has to be independent; otherwise, he will appear weak to his wife. She will lose respect for him not only as her husband, but as a man. He has to appear strong, because he is the head of the household, the leader. It's all right for his wife to be emotionally and financially dependent on him, but he must not be dependent on her. He has to take care of *everyone*. The marriage fantasy teaches the man that everyone must be able to rely on him to be strong, never passive or dependent.

4. *The good husband should be responsible for everything except the domestic part of having a family.*

The good husband should be responsible for all the so-called masculine chores around the house, like cutting the grass, fixing the car, and making sure that all mechanical things in and around the home are working right. He may not be able to do these chores himself—although these skills make him more "masculine"—but seeing that they are done is his responsibility. His main responsibility, however, is to make sure that he supports his family by working at his job outside of the home, meeting every family member's economic needs. Everything else the man does for the family is considered extra. The good husband is responsible for providing for his wife both physically (that is, making sure she has both shelter and food) and emotionally. He feels responsible when she is unhappy and depressed, and he believes that it is his duty to rescue her from any and all trouble—even when that trouble is in the realm of her own feelings or self-development. Whatever problems she is having, those problems are the good husband's responsibility, and he must find solutions so she will not feel hurt, frustrated, or angry.

5. *The good husband should have the final say in all decision-making processes in the marriage.*

At all times—according to the marriage fantasy—the good husband must be the leader in the family. (A few years ago, Archie Bunker, on the television program "All In The Family," expressed this idea in a succinct though characteristically comic fashion when he told his wife Edith that "the husband is the president of the family, even though nobody didn't vote for him.") Although he may delegate some of his power, he must never relinquish it. In reality, he may not be the leader, but it should look that way to outsiders. If outsiders ever perceived that the situation might be otherwise, the man could lose their respect, and that would be damaging to his ego. The man should be made to feel that he is better suited than his wife for making decisions because he is wiser and more knowledgeable than she about the world outside of their home.

6. *The good husband should be in control of himself most of the time.*

The last thing a good husband should ever do is "lose his cool"— that is, become emotional, silly, foolish, or illogical. The good husband is taught to look upon such behavior as a sign of weakness and vulnerability—something he must avoid at all cost. He has to be in control of himself so that his wife can lean on him. She must be able to count on his steadiness to get them through the emotional rough spots. It is as though the mere fact that he has gotten married makes him mature, a man of responsibility. Thereafter he should project an adult, controlled exterior, with no visible childlike behavior.

He must control his emotions, "ride herd" on them at all times, so they don't control him. At least, that's what he thinks. He needs to be in control so that he can stay calm and logical while he solves any emotional conflicts that may occur between himself and his wife. If he were to lose control of his emotions, he would lose his objectivity and not be able to understand their problems or how to solve them.

7. *The good husband should strive for materialistic accumulation as his source of status and identity.*

The more material wealth a man gives to his family, the better he will be judged as a provider and a husband. So he devotes most of his time and energy to this pursuit. In the suburbs of America, there are certain minimal standards he should meet: a good car (preferably two), a comfortable house, all his family members dressed in currently popular styles, and a general living standard at least equal to that of his neighbors.

A good husband believes that other people judge him by his performance and achievement in his business or profession, and the evidence of his success in these areas is reflected in his material possessions. At all times, he must compete with other men to prove his status in his community. Since material objects are the symbols of his success, the proof that he is "winning the race," their accumulation is extremely high on his list of priorities.

8. The good husband should defend his opinion and fight to win, for he should be competitive.

If the good husband isn't aggressive or doesn't fight to win, he runs the risk of losing his wife's respect. He needs to show everyone who's boss, in his own marriage as well as in all other relationships. The worst thing he can imagine is that other people might think that he is henpecked or that he doesn't "run the whole show" in his family.

Again and again, I have watched men try to live up to these goals—sometimes with tragic results. Men succeed in their role as good husbands to varying degrees, but the cost to them as human beings is almost always high, both physically and psychologically. The more the man tries to fulfill his prescribed good husband role, the less and less he knows what and who he is. In trying to be a good husband, he frequently becomes dehumanized, a robot operating on orders from a remote transmitter outside himself.

The Split Before the Split

The good husband puts himself in a schizophrenic position when he actually makes an effort to avoid bringing his work problems home with him. To keep these two worlds separate for very long is impossible, mainly beause the emotions that he experiences at work do not just go away when he walks through the door of his house at the end of the day. He may be able to mask or repress his feelings with a couple of drinks, for example, but eventually his feelings will make themselves known. The emotions he is trying to repress will contaminate his behavior and his mood for the rest of the evening. He may not be aware of what's causing his behavior, because to admit that he was bringing home work problems would mean he wasn't being a good husband.

Another set of problems present themselves when the good husband goes to work after a fight with his wife. He finds it hard to keep his mind on his job. He may be irritable with fellow workers or generally unmotivated. It's hard for him to dull his feelings at work. He can't drink or use other drugs because to do so would affect his work and cause other people to notice that all was not well with him. Some corporations, however, have realized that an employee's home life can affect that individual's productivity and have established programs to identify and assist troubled employees. In some ways, these corporations are ahead of the rest of us in recognizing that family life and industry are intertwined. Together, home and work make up the good husband's whole experience. If he fragments this experience by trying to separate work from home life, he lays the groundwork for self-alienation and becomes subject to such emotional or physical health problems as alcoholism and drug abuse, as well as the more acceptable stress diseases (ulcers and digestive disorders, heart disease, and so forth).

When the good husband does not share his work experiences with his wife, he cheats both his wife and himself. She is unable to get a picture of what he does at his job, and so there is a whole part of him that she never gets to know. He denies himself an opportunity to get his job-related problems "off his chest" and possibly find answers to these problems. Finally, what is he to talk about if not his job? Most men are interested in the work they do and find it exciting to talk about. The man who feels he shouldn't talk about his job may resort to making conversation with subject matter that interests him very little—a boring prospect at best.

So many of the elements of the good-husband fantasy are unworkable that it is difficult to know where to begin a discussion of them. The role of the good husband is especially sad when the man becomes a white knight who tries, time and again, to rescue his wife from herself. He will fail, time and again, to save her, because the truth is that only she can rescue herself from her problems. Although she may send out signals that she wants his help, she resents it when it comes. Seeing his wife as the fair damsel in distress, the good-husband knight comes dashing in on his great white steed, and every time, just as he gets to the point of saving her, he gets knocked down. He tries again and again, but the same thing always happens. Then, after a series of failures, something very peculiar occurs: he begins to blame his own object of love for his distress and attacks the damsel for being the cause of his terrible frustrations.

The nice, caring, rescuing husband, who started off with such good intentions, ends up persecuting his wife for being a victim, for being the needy soul who once provided him with such a wonderful opportunity to be heroic. The irony is that his own efforts contribute to her upset state of mind. After all, why should she change when she gets all that attention from him by staying the way she is? Taken one step further, he needs her to need him. Even if the attention she gets from him is negative, at least it is intense and sincere. I have watched such relationships continue in the same way for years, in part because the roles played by husband and wife are interwoven in such a complex pattern. But, as I have told many couples in my work, it only takes one of them to break that pattern.

Some husbands blame themselves rather than their wives for their failed rescue attempts. Such a man feels inadequate because he is unable to "help" his wife. The frustration, guilt, and anger that grow out of his sense of inadequacy are repressed and turn into depression. Because he can't stand to have his inner wounds aggravated by reminders of his inadequacy, he withdraws from his wife and puts his energy into activities that don't involve her, such as his work or a hobby—or he may just withdraw emotionally. If he stays in this emotionally withdrawn state, he may become the victim.

In his withdrawn state, the good husband isn't a lot of fun. On weekends, he is too tired to enjoy recreation, or he has a lot of things to take care of—a list that never seems to end. He puts his marriage on "hold" for some future date when there will be time to get back to it. But that time may never come unless he liberates himself from the fantasy that triggered his withdrawal.

Good husbands can find a variety of excuses for not talking to their wives about their jobs. I often hear husbands say they don't want their wives to worry. On the surface, this seems like a thoughtful gesture, but when it is further explored, most couples discover that the good husband is really following that part of his marriage fantasy which tells him that women don't have the capacities for handling masculine problems. When a man adopts this position—consciously or not—he comes to believe that he must carry the whole load alone. He can't ask his wife for support, for if he did, he wouldn't be a good husband. In addition, he usually cannot share his burden with fellow workers since he is often in competition with them and cannot allow them to see his vulnerable spots. His resentment and anxiety may disrupt his marriage, impair his performance on the job, and cause both emotional and physical disease.

The good husband may avoid disclosing work-related problems to his wife because he believes that she would simply not understand them. In order to examine the fallacy of this belief, let's look at a particular couple—Tom and Nancy Aikman, a nuclear physicist and his wife. Tom is having a problem with an experiment at the lab, but he doesn't want to tell his wife about it because, he says, she wouldn't understand the problem or be able to do anything about it. After all, he argues, she has never studied nuclear physics and can hardly be expected to know anything about it. So why tell her, right? Wrong! I explain to Tom that although Nancy may not understand nuclear physics, she can understand what it's like to feel pressure, anxiety, frustration, and the fear of failure. She has felt these feelings herself and can empathize with them. For regardless of their formal knowledge, ethnic background, or social position, all people have this one thing in common—their feelings.

And while it is true that Tom Aikman's wife may not be able to shed light on the problem he's having with his experiment, Tom may find that, after sharing his frustrations with her, he is able to go back to his work feeling more relaxed, with a clear and open mind, and solve the problem himself.

The Man's Rewards for Being a Good Husband

By not letting himself be dependent on his wife or anyone else, the good husband sets himself up for failure and a variety of potentially debilitating emotional conflicts. To begin with, he creates counterdependency—meaning that the more he tries to avoid becoming dependent on his wife, the more he deepens his dependency. The dependency in this case is emotional, rather than financial or physical. He fools himself into believing that he doesn't need anyone, particularly not his wife, so he can be "strong" and alone—the macho-hero type. The irony is that he can do this *only if* his wife is right there by his side—figuratively speaking—playing the role of the good wife, giving him the security of her emotional support. She fills a big void that he creates through his behavior, a void that he may not ever be able to see if she plays her role well. More often, however, the man and woman play their roles imperfectly, and the good husband simply refuses to admit his needs.

The good husband is often a person who never learned how to take care of himself emotionally. He generally expects a woman to do this for him—his mother, his girlfriend, or his wife. She is there as his emotional security blanket, providing security that he seldom acknowledges. Indeed, he rarely, if ever, expresses any appreciation for her emotional support.

Though he is seldom aware of it, the good husband resents being emotionally dependent on his wife, and this resentment rises to the surface in ways that cause anxiety for everyone. One common way in which a man may express his resentment is by adopting an attitude of indifference toward his family, taking his relationship with his wife for granted. He gives more time and energy to other people and other activities than he gives to his wife. It's amost as though he is testing her devotion to him by seeing how far he can push her away before she threatens him with leaving. Then he is ready to do anything to get her to stay, to make everything between them right again. When he starts to feel secure again—assuming they have succeeded to some degree in reconciling their marriage—he may repeat the process all over again. The danger is that he may push too far too often and one day find that there is nothing he can do to bring back his wife and restore his emotional security blanket. When she withdraws emotionally from him, he becomes acutely aware of his dependency— though his awareness may still not be fully conscious—and usually becomes emotionally distant, full of the feelings that he has generally suppressed, such as anger, hurt, fear, and loneliness. He may drink heavily in an attempt to numb these emotions, or he may become depressed and lethargic. In a very real way, these are the symptoms of a man going through a psychological and physical withdrawal from his addiction to his wife's emotional support. She is no longer supplying him with that "emotional fix" he so desparately needs, and like the drug addict, he must live the symptoms of withdrawal before he kicks the habit—or finds a new supplier. He feels a deep need for his wife, and yet, at the same time, he resents needing her so much.

The good husband's fantasy that he shouldn't be dependent on others cannot help but lower his sense of self-esteem. The good husband will eventually find himself stuck in a double bind. He believes he must never be weak, and he sees any dependency as a weakness. At the same time, he feels tremendous stress at having always to be strong. And the sad thing is that the good husband rarely sees the bind he's in. He ends up feeling inadequate, as a husband and as a man, to meet a self-imposed set of standards, perhaps unknown to him, no one can satisfactorily fulfill.

The White Knight Trapped in His Armor

A good husband is responsible for his wife's well-being. He is her protection and support. This part of the good-husband fantasy sets the man up for emotional as well as physical problems. If the woman has not liberated herself from the good-wife fantasy, she may, in fact, act passive and dependent, feeling threatened by the idea of being responsible for herself. Her behavior seems to justify the man's belief that he must take care of his wife—but does it? When he takes responsibility for her, he deprives her of the opportunity to learn how to care for herself and thus maintains her dependence. In my experience, the man's need to be responsible for his wife is not based so much on necessity or desirability as it is on the good-husband fantasy to which he subscribes.

Although the stress and anxiety he feels may not be acceptable to the man, the good husband's fantasy is that "he should be able to handle the job." So he tries to repress his feelings, but the feelings don't go away—they just go underground. Medical researchers have demonstrated that repressed or controlled feelings actually cause physical changes in a person's body, changes in the antibody system (which makes that person less able to resist infections), changes in stomach secretions (causing ulcers or chronic indigestion), and even changes in the blood vessels (causing heart disease). In addition, stress and anxiety cause hormonal changes that can result in an actual reduction in energy and cause a depression that is not just a transitory mood, but a very real physiological state.

The list of problems upon which the good husband can focus his rescue missions is an endless one. If his wife is feeling depressed, he believes he is responsible for getting her out of her depression. If she is not having orgasms, he believes he is responsible for that. In his mind, he is responsible for taking care of his wife both physically and emotionally until, as the marriage vow states, "death do us part." The only problem with this noble viewpoint is that it is not realistic. It is almost impossible to be responsible for another person's feelings and behavior. Everyone has normal ups and downs, but when his wife is on a down cycle, the white knight character is engaged in the good husband and sets out to rescue her. She may not have ever requested his help, but by now both parties are convinced it is necesary. Maintaining the posture of all the other dictates of the good-husband role, the man buys his wife a new dress, a new car, or a house in a better neighborhood. Yet he begins to notice that all these efforts don't produce any change in her, except that maybe she wants more. When she does feel better, it only lasts a short time. So he must continually supply her with new diversions and new *stuff* to keep her happy.

At this point, another irony enters the picture. Because more things is not what she ultimately needs to make her feel better, the wife becomes disturbed by her husband's inability to help her. Although she will not be aware of it if she is playing her good-wife role as it is supposed to be played, the source of her anger lies not in her husband's failure to supply her with enough things, but in his failure to give her the personal attention and intimacy they may have enjoyed in their courtship. As a result, she may now change her role from helpless victim to attacking persecutor.

As long as he is limited to the good-husband fantasy, a man will place an inordinate amount of importance on his ability to help his wife with her problems. The trouble is that if she gets better or ceases to need his help, he's out of a job—at least, in his own mind. It is as though he were saying to his wife: "I want you to get better, or become more independent and not be such a helpless victim, but I still want you to need me." Thus, a man may help his wife find a solution to a problem, then turn right around and sabotage that solution so that she must return to him for more help. Such patterns of behavior may seem obvious when described here, but they are seldom obvious when we are living them out in real life because we are usually following marriage fantasies of which we are only vaguely aware.

The 60/40 Arrangement

The good-husband fantasy requires that the man be the decision-maker in the family. From the first day of his marriage, he feels compelled to establish and maintain his dominance. It is a never-ending struggle, one aggravated by his competitive stance and other aspects of his good-husband fantasy.

Not the least of his troubles arises from the fact that, as the person at the top, he must always be on his guard, protecting his position from others who (he is certain) think just as he does and want to topple him from his throne. By putting himself in the top position, the good husband not only creates resentment in his wife, who may feel her husband does not respect her, but also experiences his own resentment. He has fought for his dominance, but then he begins to resent the burden of responsibility that comes with being head of the house.

Constantly seeking to maintain his position, the good husband never lets down his guard. He slowly becomes alienated from himself as well as his wife. As the old saying goes, "It's lonely at the top." Having no real emotional interaction with his wife and probably only superficial emotional contact with others at work, the good husband finds himself increasingly isolated from other people.

Being the head of the family works for the good husband only as long as his wife allows him to have that authority. The reality in today's world is that fewer and fewer women are willing to go along with the game. Too often this creates a power struggle in the marriage. The good husband is then forced into combat with his wife, who, in his eyes, has ceased to be a good wife. If the situation is carried to its logical conclusion, the good husband becomes "the heavy," forcing his wife to accept his ideas through sheer force, threats, or manipulations—all the tactics of war. He may realize his machinations aren't scoring many points with his wife, but his ego may be bolstered and, for the time being, that's enough for him. If he chooses to let down his guard and go along with his wife (rather than continue to dominate her), he may begin to lose self-esteem. His wife may not resent him as much then, and may even feel emotionally closer to him, but he may feel ambivalent. And his ambivalence may be supported by mixed messages from his wife, who may want a dominating husband in some situations and an equal, or even subservient, partner in others. These mixed messages often confuse the man and complicate his efforts to change his good-husband fantasies.

The good-husband fantasy is packed with so many contradictions that it is all but impossible for the good husband to feel good about himself. His confusion creates insecurity, anxiety, and tension for him, which in themselves put pressure on the relationship. Many a man reacts by becoming very steadfast or even rigid in his role as head of the family. Some even take pride in being labeled "male chauvinist pigs." All too often, a man who takes this reactionary stance permanently alienates his spouse, and she decides to dissolve their marriage. He will usually recognize how his stance contributed to the breakup—but only after the split.

The Husband as Parent to His Wife

When the man takes the position of being the boss, or head of the household, he creates a kind of parent relationship with his wife.

He becomes an authority over her, just as her father probably was. Most adult women resent being treated as children in this way. Although, in the beginning, a woman may feel a certain amount of security in being married to a man who assumes such a role, after a while her subtle resentments may grow into a full-blown rage. The good husband is then marked as her target.

If she was properly following the guidelines provided by the good-wife marriage fantasy, she would have been encouraging him to assume a strong stance and take care of her—as a good husband should. To encourage him, she would have played helpless. But even the woman who starts out that way ordinarily tires of her subservience and begins to grow up very quickly. If, for example, she gets a job outside the home where she functions as an adult and is respected as one, she may begin to notice, and resent, the way she is treated at home. Her resentment quickly surfaces in the marriage since she wants to be treated as a capable adult by her husband. The man who doesn't recognize this, and who persists in his good-husband, head-of-the-household role, is well on his way to the divorce court.

The same pattern changes can occur in a marriage when the husband and wife are separated for an extended period of time. Since she cannot go running to him for answers and advice, she soon takes total responsibility for herself. And when her husband returns, he finds a different woman, one who is more independent and self-assured. This changed situation may create tension and conflict between the couple, unless the husband is willing and able to change his behavior to stay up with his wife's growth. For example, a GI returning from war may find quite a different woman than he married a couple of years earlier.

While a woman may resent her husband acting like a parent, a man may also resent having to act like a father to the woman he married. He may resent her dependence because he is already having a difficult time taking care of himself and wants someone to take care of *him*. In this case, both partners may become locked in a battle to try to get each other to take responsibility for the household or, on a subtler level, the man's resentment—almost like sibling rivalry—will widen the gap between himself and his wife.

Most men in our culture think they must be in control of themselves at all times. But the primary problem with this attitude is that it goes against human nature. Since it is impossible to be in control emotionally all the time, the good husband is almost guaranteed to fail, at least in his own eyes.

Anyone who attempts to maintain control at all times is doomed to become an up-tight, boring person. His vitality, his spirit is always held in check. He loses all positive childlike qualities, such as spontaneity and excitement. He turns into a robot just going through the motions of being alive. The only time he is able to let go is when he is stoned or drunk.

The good husband tries to hold himself in check because he is afraid he will otherwise become controlled by his feelings. Ironically, the more he tries to control his emotions, the more he comes under their control. He lives in fear of his feelings coming out (because sometimes they do, as when he loses his temper), and so he tries harder and harder to control his emotions. I like the analogy of the Dutch boy trying to plug up the holes in the dike: eventually, he just runs out of fingers to stop the leaks, and before he knows it, he is engulfed in water.

The good husband may try to anesthetize his feelings when they become too intense for him to repress. He may come home from a hard day at the office and head straight for the liquor cabinet to fix himself a drink. Alcohol does take the edge off the day's tensions and anxieties, but at the same time, it numbs his feelings for his wife and family. This whole process may backfire on the good husband. If he drinks too much, he may lose control of all his emotions, all the feelings he has been trying to hold back. The emotions, unleashed under the influence of alcohol, can be very destructive. And, of course, with every alcohol-induced blowup, he becomes further convinced that it is necessary to control what he feels, and this makes alcohol increasingly important to him.

When the Materialistic Dream Turns Sour

Striving for material wealth is an important part of the good-husband fantasy. The man's self-esteem—if he is being guided by the marriage fantasy—is built on his ability to earn a decent salary and "provide for his family." There is nothing wrong with being a good provider, but when that priority is put above all others, problems definitely do arise. The American Dream then becomes a nightmare.

In my practice as a marriage counselor, it is common for me to hear a wife tell her husband how much happier she was when they were first married, before they had so much money. Of course, this is hindsight, and the same wife will readily admit that she was right beside her husband, encouraging him in promotions that would increase his workload or require him to travel and be away from the family for extended periods. They both were excited by the prospect of having more money, of being able to buy things that would make their lives more comfortable or interesting.

But all too often the dream turns sour. Though the husband earns more money and purchases the things that he and his wife always dreamed of enjoying, they now have become strangers to each other, and no matter how wonderful the things they own, their wealth cannot compensate them for the loneliness they feel.

I remember one woman—I'll call her Joan—who came to see me because she was having an affair with a man she'd met at a neighborhood party. She felt terribly guilty about the affair. As she put it, "I know my husband works hard and I do appreciate what he's trying to do, but I never see him anymore. He comes home, but by the time he gets there, he's burned out. He has no time or energy for *us* anymore. He eats dinner, hardly tastes his food, has a couple of drinks, watches television, and goes to bed. He's there, all right, but he might as well be a million miles away. I feel like a widow."

In Joan's case, her loneliness drove her to seek affection and emotional attention from another man. She felt doubly guilty about this because she had wanted material wealth as much as her husband did. In fact, she still wanted it, but in the end, she came to the conclusion that the accumulation of things was not worth sacrificing her husband's emotional life. At this point, they began to make changes in their marriage.

When the American Dream is taken to its outer limits, there is often a kind of existential breakdown among men who have followed the good-husband fantasy to the letter and have gotten to the top of their particular corporate ladders. Such a man finds that having achieved his goal of buying a boat or a new house no longer gives his life meaning. As Herb Goldberg points out in *The New Male*: "In the end, the rewards of his success are revealed as masturbatory. There is really no one to share them with when he gets 'there,' no one close enough who really cares or knows him and whom he genuinely trusts and feels close to." One man once said to me, "Well, I have everything I worked hard for all my life. Yet, I keep thinking there must be something more to life!" This client was depressed and withdrawn in his marriage. He had lost his "zest for life." Some refer to this change in values as "male menopause." Whatever label we give these feelings, they arise because a basic premise of the good-husband fantasy has started to lose its meaning. The man may have to change his belief about what is important, if he wishes to find new meaning in his life. In the words of Herb Goldberg again, "While achievement and accomplishment are important for a sense of self-worth in most people, the success-driven man has substituted the acquisition of symbols for human intimacy and satisfaction."

The High Cost of Winning

In the hard competitive environment of the marketplace, the good husband's ability to fight and win may spell the difference between failure and success in his career. When he carries home the need to win—as he will—that need continues to make the difference between failure and success, but in a markedly different way. Though he may not be aware that he is bringing his competitive skills and impulses into his marriage, they severely limit his relationship with his wife.

The good husband pays a high emotional price for having to

win or always be right in his marriage. The aggressive behavior that works so well for him in his pursuit of money may alienate his wife. If someone has to be right, then someone else must be wrong. If someone wins, then someone else loses. In this case, the someone who loses is usually the good wife. But no one likes losing and being wrong, and the wife starts to feel resentment toward her husband. This resentment may not be expressed immediately, since the good wife wants her husband to feel he is the boss, so that together they can fulfill the marriage fantasy. However, as we have already seen, feelings must get expressed one way or another. Eventually, the resentment she has been stuffing erupts, usually in some hurtful manner and usually directed toward the good husband.

A basic problem with the good husband's need to win and be right is that he becomes a terrible listener, unable to really understand his wife's position and emotions. He cuts her off or puts her down, often not even aware of his effect on her. As a result, she may stop coming to him for any meaningful conversation. She feels alienated from him. His need to be on top pushes away the very person who is best able to nourish his emotional side.

The need to be right and to win all the time puts tremendous pressure on the good husband to strive for perfection in his performance. In his own mind, he feels he must always know the right answer. He must never look bad. But humans, unlike machines, are never perfect. In his efforts to make himself look good, the man pays more attention to his defensive skills than to what he really wants or needs out of life. Those defensive skills are so important in the marketplace that one large corporation is now giving their top management people something called C.Y.A. classes. C.Y.A. stands for "Covering Your Ass."

Looking right even when you are wrong is a false front, of course. However, the ability to erect this false front can be an essential skill to one who is climbing the corporate ladder, arguing a case in court, or demanding respect as a construction boss. Unfortunately, the man who applies this skill to every aspect of his life will ultimately become the loser. No one, including his wife and children, will ever get to know who he really is. And what is even more detrimental, he will never get to know himself.

The emotional wear and tear on such a man is astronomical. The feelings that all humans have within them build up pressure from within as his real self tries, again and again, to make itself known. At the same time, he feels pressure from the outside to maintain or even strengthen his facade. Like walls pressing closer and closer together, the two forces at last close in on him. Mental breakdowns, alcoholism, and heart attacks head the list of possible consequences. Somehow it is all reminiscent of a Batman matinee. With seemingly unconquerable forces bearing down from all sides, nothing short of a miracle can save our hero now.

Of course, many men caught up in this kind of trap never escape for any number of reasons. They may become too rigid and defensive to admit they might benefit from change. Or, they may have already so alienated their wives that there is no chance of them regaining their love, no matter how they change for the better. Yet, with the good-wife fantasy, awareness of the trap and an understanding of its dimensions is the first step toward freedom.

Exercise No. 1: Husband/Wife "Should" Lists

PURPOSE: To clarify your definitions and your mate's definitions of good-wife/good-husband fantasies.

PREPARATION: Make room for approximately one hour of uninterrupted time with your mate. Have a paper and pencil on hand for taking notes.

EXERCISE: Both you and your mate make two lists—one outlining what you feel a good husband should do or be, and the other outlining what you feel a good wife should do or be. If you wish, refer to the good-wife/good-husband rules given in chapters three and four to help you get started. List everything you can think of, no matter how obvious or mundane you may think it is.

1) Compare your lists with those of your mate.

2) Discuss how your lists are similar—or how they differ.

3) Discuss alterations you and your mate have made in the past. (For example, discuss how the husband's attention to his family

may have been affected by increased work responsibilities, or
how a wife's attention to her family was changed when she went
to work outside the home.)

4) Discuss changes you both might make to improve your relationship or alter your marriage fantasy.

5. Feelings Are the Facts of Intimacy

Now that we've looked at the marriage fantasy and have discussed some of the potential pitfalls of good-husband and good-wife roles, let's move on to explore how a couple can immediately start enjoying emotional intimacy again. As we begin this part of the book, I'd like you to keep in mind that there are no rights or wrongs here. There is only what works or what doesn't work—and you and your mate will be the final judges of that.

Begin with Feelings

Whenever I work with a couple in counseling, the first thing we look at is how much feeling exists in the relationship. Feelings—both positive and negative ones—are the lifeblood of a marriage. It is the flow of feeling that keeps marriage exciting, vibrant, and growing.

What are the feelings that keep a relationship alive? Anger, hurt, pride, sadness, guilt, anxiety, joy, excitement, hatred, resentment, concern, contentment, pressure, tension, elation, appreciation—these are only a few of the many human feelings we all experience in our lives. So when I use the word *feeling* I am not talking about thoughts or ideas or opinions, but sensations you feel largely in your body. Although thoughts may be involved, one experiences feeling mostly as physical sensation.

Feelings Are Always Real

There is one basic premise that I always try to keep in mind when working with couples in counseling: *Whatever feeling a person is experiencing is an irrefutable fact for that person.* When a woman feels angry about something her husband did, that anger is real for her, regardless of the circumstances that may have provoked it. The anger is a complex physiological event occurring inside her. It is a physical reality.

Although one might have the best of intentions, trying to talk a person out of his or her feelings usually causes more problems than it solves. For example, to say to the person who feels angry, "You shouldn't feel that way," or "What are you so upset about?" has the effect of denying that person's feelings. It's like telling someone that he or she has the wrong color of eyes or shouldn't be as tall or as short as they are.

Even though a person's anger makes no sense and seems to have no *logical* or *rational* foundation, the feeling is still reality for the person experiencing it. The first step toward emotional intimacy in a marriage is accepting your mate's feelings as fact, as something that is never up for debate.

Many people find it difficult to accept their own feelings, much less those of another person. All of us have this problem to one degree or another, and so we say to ourselves, "I shouldn't let that bother me," or "It's just a little, silly, trite, petty issue," or "Why rock the boat? Things are going so smoothly right now." Often these are reflex responses, but they can lead to the repression or denial of your feelings. As you become increasingly successful at talking yourself out of your feelings of anger or resentment, you will find it becomes increasingly difficult to express feelings of love for your mate.

Repressed feelings don't go away. Instead, they get boxed up. You may think that you don't have a particular feeling any more, but the truth is that it is still there, lying dormant like a seed, waiting for the opportunity to come alive again, perhaps in a different form, perhaps as a physical ailment. A myth in our society is that if an individual ignores, avoids, denies, rationalizes, or holds back his or her feelings, these feelings will go away and no longer bother the person.

A good example of how this works might begin with John doing something like forgetting his wife Jane's birthday. As a result of his forgetfulness, Jane feels very hurt, angry, and disappointed with John. What John does is to tell her, "I'm sorry, it's in the *past*, so why don't you forget about it, and let's have a good time *now*. There is nothing I can do about it at this point anyway. I'll make it up to you next year." Jane's feelings are not eradicated by John's apology. In fact, she gets more upset than ever with him and walks off in bewilderment. She may attempt to bring up the subject repeatedly—sometimes again and again over a period of years— only to have John tell her the same thing every time.

What happens is that every time Jane tries to express her feelings about the forgotten birthday, John asks her to deny or repress what she feels. The husband may not be able to understand why his wife's anger continues as the result of something that happened long ago. But the truth is that although the incident that provoked her anger is long past, Jane's feelings are very much in the present. As he struggles for an explanation, John may accuse Jane of bringing up the subject again and again to punish him. But that isn't what she's doing either. Jane is compelled by something far more basic and personal than that: recognition, or an acknowledgment of her feelings.

Holding Back Can Go Too Far

Somehow we've gotten the idea that we can hold back *some* feelings and yet continue to feel free to express others. But in my practice it becomes clear that once the emotional door is closed on *some* feelings, it gets closed on *all* of them. Furthermore, no matter how you lean against that door, trying to seal in your feelings, some feelings still get out, but they probably will have lost a lot of their intensity and energy in the process. This is true of both negative feelings, such as hurt, anger, and resentment, and positive feelings, such as appreciation, care, and love. To go back to Jane, John, and the forgotten birthday issue: if Jane does not express her resentment to John, this feeling will become harder and harder to live with until she finds it all but impossible to express her feelings of caring and appreciation. But people are never one hundred percent successful at hiding their feelings. Sometimes, when you don't expect it, the emotional door slips ajar, and the unexpressed feelings slip through.

A common way the door comes open is during sex. Let's say a couple has just made love and they're feeling good about each other. They feel close and satisfied. Then, suddenly, the woman begins to cry. The husband is confused, and the woman herself doesn't understand what is happening. But the explanation is really quite simple. During the expression of sexual feelings, especially when the person relinquishes conscious control enough to enjoy orgasm, he or she releases other feelings as well. The woman who cries after intercourse, or the man who instantly turns away may be feeling sadness, fear, or even guilt, originally stimulated long ago by an event that may have had nothing to do with the present sexual experience.

So, to go back to our example, if Jane starts to express her caring feelings to John, starts to open the emotional door, the resentment and anger she's been holding back may also want to come out. But because she is afraid of these "bad" feelings, she makes a great effort to hold them back, and in the process, she also holds back her caring feelings. As a result, she ends up expressing little emotion of any kind, limiting her intimacy with John.

Just as feelings are to be considered facts, so are they to be considered neither right nor wrong, good nor bad, negative nor positive. A feeling is just a feeling. Accept it. When people judge their own feelings, or when they judge the feelings of someone else with whom they are emotionally intimate, they block the expression of something that needs to come out. If the atmosphere in a marriage is one of judgment, it isn't emotionally safe to express feelings. If someone judges your feelings, you will most likely feel hurt. To evaluate a feeling with such phrases as, "Oh, it's stupid to feel angry about that," or "That's silly, dumb, or petty," discounts or devalues that emotion. Remember, the feeling is a fact, and there is a reason for its existence.

Emotion is a signal felt in your body, telling you to do something. The message may be a simple or an obvious one, as in the case of feeling a pin prick. The person's body is saying, "Do whatever is necessary to stop this pain." If the person tries to ignore, repress, or negate the feeling of pain, their physical well-being may be placed in jeopardy. It's like the red light flashing on the dashboard of your car, telling you that the engine needs oil. If the driver ignores the message, he may ruin the engine. If the driver responds to the message and does something to correct the problem, then everything will be fine.

Of course, feelings are not always as easy to understand and fix as the flashing light on the dashboard. A feeling of being uncomfortable or anxious is a complex message. Knowing how to respond to this kind of a message may seem quite beyond your ability to understand why you feel as you do. Nevertheless, your body is telling you something. If you ignore this message, you may regret it later.

Many people impose an unconscious rule on themselves that they must know why they feel a certain way before they can express that feeling. Frequently, this approach causes them to hold back indefinitely because they never satisfactorily answer the question of why they feel as they do. It is hard to see or think clearly when there is so much feeling in the way. Indeed, when the feeling is eventually expressed, the person's thinking actually improves. It is not unusual to see people in my practice who have become so confused and frustrated trying to figure out a feeling that they've completely lost touch with the original feeling that got them started on their intellectual quest. What happens then is similar to what happens when you struggle to remember someone's name. You try, but it just doesn't come. Finally you give up and relax. Ten minutes later, the name seems to pop right into your consciousness. Many times feelings behave the same way. You may feel uncomfortable and anxious about something, but when someone asks why you feel as you do, you draw a blank. It is helpful to know that if you acknowledge the feeling and verbally express it as well as you can, the cause or source will, in time, become clear.

Energy and Feelings

Another rationale used for not communicating feelings is expressed in such phrases as, "It won't do any good," or "It won't change anything." This rationale is especially common among men, and while it's true that the expression of feelings may not produce change in a person's physical environment, it does produce change in a person's inner self in ways that are both physical and emotional. Feelings contain physiological energy. They may vary in intensity depending on what they are and who is feeling them. But when this emotional energy is held back, the person begins to feel drained. Not only is energy going to the original feeling, but more energy is being consumed in the effort to control that feeling. After expressing feelings in an appropriate and satisfying way, a person's internal tension is released, energy is released, and the person feels better. Many times, after expressing feelings with someone listening, he or she ends up feeling a lot better. Nothing may have changed at home, but something has surely happened. The person suddenly has infinitely more energy to deal with the problems at hand and enjoy his or her life more.

Feelings Form Important Foundations

In most marriages, certain judgments of emotional states are expressed again and again. These judgments are expressed in such phrases as, "You are being overemotional" and "You are just too sensitive about that." These judgments, though they may seem true to the person expressing them, inhibit the expression of feelings. What the person making these statements communicates to the other person is, "Your feelings are out of scale to what's actually happened, so stop expressing yourself." But remember, feelings are fact. The origin of these feelings may have nothing to do with the incident that the person expressing judgments assumes was the source of provocation. Instead, their origin may be related to something that happened in the distant past. But all of us live partly in the past, and the feelings that come out of it are real.

It is much better for an "overemotional" spouse to be given his or her chance to express the feelings that come up, even if their intensity doesn't fit the current situation. After the discharge of emotional energy, the true source of the emotional intensity will often become clear. At this point, hopefully, the real issue and its related feelings may be resolved for good.

One important concept related to feelings is that they are to be trusted when we are dealing with areas of our life where there doesn't seem to be a well-defined sense of what is right and wrong. Whenever you are faced with problems where there is no well-defined sense of what is wrong and right, trust what you feel. I have kicked myself many times for not trusting my own feelings.

Feelings are a guide in uncharted territory. Usually they are the best guide because so much of our rational thought is mixed up with other people's ideas, attitudes, or beliefs that they may be right for them, but not right for us. Any time there is a tough decision to be made, our emotions are an accurate barometer to help us make the best choice.

In marriage, it is important for partners to trust each other's feelings in the same way as they trust their own. Let's say that John asks his wife, "Do you want to go skiing this weekend?" Jane replies, "I'm not sure." Wanting very much to go, John says, "Why not? It would be a great weekend. I hear there's new snow and the exercise would do us both good." Jane is probably confused at this point. She hears the logic of John's argument, but is feeling uncomfortable or just not very enthusiastic about going. She is not sure why she doesn't want to go—she just doesn't. If she buys John's logical sales pitch and goes skiing, ignoring her own feelings, they may both regret later that they went. The reason she wasn't enthusiastic to begin with may become painfully evident when they get there, but by then it's too late. She is already committed. Because she doesn't want to be there, she may begin to resent being talked into going, and this creates obvious tension between her and John, tension that may get in the way of either one of them enjoying themselves. If, on the other hand, she talks about her feelings as they relate to the ski trip, and John listens without trying to judge or talk her out of her feelings through the use of logic and persuasion, Jane may well get in touch with her own feelings. Once the source is found, the feeling can usually be resolved and a decision made that will work to the benefit of both husband and wife.

Build Awareness of Feelings

What if a person does not know what he or she is feeling? This is often the case with the men I see in my counseling. In order to communicate how one feels, one must first become aware of what one is feeling. Until this awareness is built, effective emotional communication is impossible.

Becoming aware of how one feels is not as easy as it sounds.

Many people develop automatic patterns to repress their awareness of feelings—even though, as I've previously said, those feelings are there. One begins to build awareness by looking not directly at the feelings themselves but at the beliefs or attitudes that
support the repression or denial of those feelings. For example, we
begin to examine statements such as: "Why talk about it? It won't
change things," "It's best to be rational and never let your emotions get the best of you," or "Feelings prove that you are vulnerable and weak," or "If I express what I really feel, it may hurt other
people." Most of these beliefs are learned in childhood, taught by
well-meaning parents who simply don't know how to teach children how to express their feelings—usually because the parents
themselves don't know how to handle their feelings. To help people see past these denial-supporting statements, I often suggest
replacing them with new beliefs, such as, "It hurts the person I
love not to tell that person how I feel," and "The more I express
my feelings, the more rational and emotionally calm I can
become."

After a person learns that there are real benefits to be gained by
learning to express feelings, old attitudes of denial fall away. Although the door to awareness is open, you may need to make a
deliberate effort to ask yourself what you are feeling. Focus on
actual body sensations. For example, the sensation of "butterflies
in the stomach" means you're feeling anxious, nervous, afraid, or
excited. Tightness in your shoulders and neck is often a feeling of
anger. Other body signals—tension, pressure, increase in pulse
rate—may indicate feelings of anger, anxiety, excitement, fear, or
fatigue.

What I would like you to remember is that feelings are real
physical events in your body. To deny them is to deny a rich and
rewarding part of your life. Acknowledging them, on the other
hand, opens you up to greater intimacy with those you love, establishing a new depth to your relationships that will come back to
you in emotional security you may have never dreamed possible.

6. The Courage to Be Vulnerable

Vulnerability is the foundation for intimacy. In this chapter, we will focus on the extent to which married people allow themselves to be vulnerable with one another. We will also discuss some of the things that may inhibit their ability to let themselves be vulnerable.

To be vulnerable in your love relationship means you are able to trust another person with information about your thoughts and feelings that would expose you to the possibility of emotional hurt. Being vulnerable is like giving someone a map of your emotional "land mines," showing that person where they are so he or she doesn't set them off by accident. Being vulnerable is indicating the area below your psychological "belt line"—that is, those parts of your life where you can be easily hurt. In casual relationships, conversation tends to focus on information that is above the psychological belt line: your work, your recreations, or other forms of activity. There's nothing wrong with these interactions, but if a marital relationship stays at that level, the chances for intimacy are slim. Being vulnerable with your spouse is like giving both of you an insurance policy against emotional injury. If Jane opens up enough to John to tell him about the things he says or does that hurt her, both partners are protected. Jane is protected because John knows what he can do to change those kinds of behavior that hurt her. John is protected because now Jane won't resent him for what he has said or done to hurt her.

When I work with two people who are just beginning to be vulnerable to each other, I tell them that a good marriage is built on weaknesses and a poor marriage is built on false strengths. I see many couples who look good, who don't fight or have conflicts. Everyone thinks such a pair has a great marriage, and then they are surprised to find out that this "happy couple" is getting a divorce.

This couple had built a nice facade, but it was hollow on the inside because the two people lacked vulnerability. Such couples usually censor out their vulnerabilities, robbing their relationships of emotional energy. These relationships are emotionally flat. There is little or no fluctuation in the emotional climate, few "ups and downs." The result is that the marital relationship becomes boring.

What prevents marriage partners from being vulnerable with one another? After all, they love each other, so why doesn't vulnerability just happen "naturally?" The answer to this question is somewhat complex, but there are several major reasons that we can examine.

The most common reason couples give for not allowing themselves to become vulnerable is that they are afraid of being hurt. This fear of being hurt usually originated when they were small children. They were vulnerable then and may have been hurt by someone close to them, perhaps a parent or sibling. They learned at an early, impressionable period of their lives that it doesn't pay to be vulnerable. Their fear may have also developed when they were dating in high school, when they were "burned" by a boyfriend or a girlfriend. Or, their fear of being hurt could stem from their current marital relationship. In the early days of their marriage, one or both of the spouses may have opened up and been hurt—seemingly in response to opening up. But regardless of how the fear began, the effect of it is always the same: real intimacy is blocked.

Another reason people give for not becoming vulnerable is that they are afraid of "losing the respect" of their spouses. Such people don't want to appear "weak," incapable, or "un-together." They are afraid their spouses will not accept them as they really are, that they will be judged unfavorably if they tell their mates about their fears and sensitivities. Along with their fear of being judged and found unacceptable comes the fear of losing their spouses' love—that is, of being rejected or abandoned. The fear of being vulnerable causes many couples to remain strangers to one another, unable to let down and be themselves, always living behind a facade of "looking good" or "having it all together."

Finally, not only do our most personal fears limit us in our loving relationships, but the sexual roles of society tend to pressure us as well into behaving in ways that limit vulnerability. This programming starts when we are very young and continues all the way up through young adulthood. Like the marriage-fantasy programming, sexual role programming is usually accomplished indirectly, almost subliminally, as children model themselves after their parents or after movie or television heroes and heroines. In some families, the programming is quite direct. Parents may tell their little boys not to cry and yet pamper the little girl who does cry. The degree to which such cultural programming influences attitudes and behavior varies from person to person, but all of us are exposed to the same messages.

Tough Guys and Lonely Wives

Men in our culture are taught not to be vulnerable. Because they have received this training, most men hear certain phrases repeated over and over in their minds, like a broken record that turns on any time they feel hurt, frightened, or insecure: "Be strong. Don't cry. Be aggressive so people won't think you're weak. Don't let your guard down. Don't be emotional. Stay on top. Be in control." These messages come from numerous sources, but the ultimate message is pretty universal: it's not manly to be vulnerable.

In elementary school, I once cried after my team lost a baseball game. It was an experience I'll never forget. Suddenly my own teammates were calling me names and saying, "Don't be such a cry baby. Dan's a sissy." And I even received the worst insult of all for a boy that age: "Only girls cry." The message was clear. I had to learn to control my feelings. In junior high school, I learned that being a man meant being "cool." I was not supposed to let anything bother me emotionally. Then came high school, where the competition for grades, making the team, or getting a date forced one to develop a mask of invulnerability. I can remember dating in high school and how hard I worked to *appear* "cool and sophisticated," while on the inside I was a nervous wreck. I was so out of touch with my emotions that I would sometimes lose touch with what was going on around me. I would drive through red lights and never even know it until my date told me what I'd done. It's too bad I wasn't secure enough then to open up and tell my date how I really felt. She probably would have openly accepted it, and we both could have relaxed and been ourselves.

After high school, some men go into military service, while the majority enter the business world directly or via college. By its nature, the military teaches men to live by the doctrine of nonvulnerability. It would be difficult to run an army on the basis of emotional awareness and self-knowledge. Emotions get in the way of the business of protecting a country or destroying an enemy. Make no mistake about it; military training really does prepare people to kill—and killing necessitates blocking some extremely basic feelings. The former sales slogan of the U.S. Marine Corps, "Join the Marines and let us make you a man," best illustrates the point, although no branch of the service has a monopoly on dehumanizing people.

Similarly, the ardent competitiveness of the business world hardly encourages vulnerability. Sometimes this point is made in obvious ways. Take, for example, the C.Y.A. ("cover your ass") classes mentioned earlier. From these classes, management personnel can learn such things as, "Don't let down and be yourself—it isn't safe. Protect yourself. Otherwise, you will get your throat cut." Because in the cutthroat world of business, vulnerability can truly become a dangerous thing. And the business world is not going to become more humanistic for a long time—if ever. People working in business need to accept this reality. But though a person may have little control over his or her work environment, still he or she can form more meaningful personal relationships at home.

The rigors of the work ethic affect different people in different ways, of course. Some find business an exciting creative outlet, while others feel beaten down by it. We do know, however, that people in the business world tend to suffer from tensions that carry over into their lives away from work. Although many corporations are now offering workshops to employees who want to avoid the dangers of their lifestyle, the stereotypical hard-driving businessman still exists.

Although a heart attack or bleeding ulcer may seem to appear suddenly one day, the disintegration of the individual's health always starts years earlier. Medical experts tell us that stress-related diseases begin when a person learns to be invulnerable, when he or she learns that it is not advantageous to communicate his or her real feelings to other people. Men especially keep their thoughts and feelings to themselves and thereby take on an additional burden of stress over and above that imposed by the challenges of everyday life. Being "manly" in this way is a kind of work in itself that consumes energy.

As we have already learned, feelings are a reality, and contrary to popular belief, they don't go away unless they get expressed. Whereas unexpressed feelings may cause resentment in marriage, they can cause quite another set of problems in the business world. Let us consider the example of a man we'll call Sam Hughes.

Sam works in a high-pressure job, eight hours a day, five days a week. While at work, he experiences many different emotions, some of which are pretty intense. One emotion he feels in particular is anxiety. But although Sam feels anxious, he does not allow himself to tell people at work about his feelings. He believes that he needs to keep up his front, to appear to have his emotions under control at all times. He comes home from work and doesn't want to tell his wife about his feelings either—maybe because he doesn't want to appear "weak" in her eyes, maybe because he wants to protect her from worry.

Being a good husband, Sam won't allow himself to express the great many feelings he feels anywhere. He represses them, thinking he can put his feelings out of his mind. He can, too, but only out of his conscious mind. They continue to live—at a subconscious level. And emotions do not like to be ignored. When the gentle taps of emotion are ignored, they start to knock a little louder to get that person to acknowledge their existence. Each time that knocking is ignored, it gets a little harder, then harder and harder until it is quite intense.

Sam begins to have indigestion. He starts taking antacids to relieve the problem, but his discomfort persists because the *reasons*

for his anxiety are not going away. As time goes by, the upset
stomach happens more often and hurts increasingly. But still Sam
ignores the feelings that are trying to get his attention. He takes
more antacids. The anxiety knocks a little harder. Sam finally gets
physically sick and goes to the doctor for help. He finds out he is
developing an ulcer. Now maybe Sam will decide to take a look at
his life, and perhaps his difficulties will end there. But that's not
the typical pattern. The typical pattern is that the doctor puts Sam
on a special diet and the causes of his stress go unchanged.

People who hold their emotions back may develop what is commonly known as a nervous condition. Their hands shake, they're
jittery, and maybe they have trouble sleeping. Instead of talking to
other people about the situations that are making them tense, they
ask their doctors for tranquilizers or they have a drink so they can
relax. Again, they are ignoring their feelings. Yes, they may feel
better after taking a couple pills or having a couple of drinks, but
the next day the nervousness returns. Some men anesthetize
themselves until they are no longer aware of what they feel physically. They live in a state of constant tension and their acquaint-
ances call them "up-tight." After a while, this constant state of
physical tightness can cause circulatory problems, high blood
pressure, severe headaches, constipation, and many more ail-
ments. If the tension continues indefinitely, the man's emotions
knock so hard on his body that they literally knock him down. It is
hard to ignore the seriousness of a heart attack. At this point, Sam
may finally acknowledge or listen to his feelings if it isn't already
too late.

The psychological state we call depression, with its characteris-
tic side effect of lack of energy, may also be related to the male's
inability to be vulnerable. It takes mental energy to hold back
emotions. The greater the feeling, the greater amount of energy
will be required to hold that feeling back. When mental energy is
expended in this manner, it is no wonder that one feels tired,
depressed, or unmotivated. The old advice to "get it off your
chest" is actually quite descriptive because when people express
their feelings, they often report sensations of being lighter, as if a
great weight had been lifted from their shoulders. They feel that

way because they are suddenly getting the benefit of energy that was being used to hold back their feelings.

Many good husbands who try to control their work-related emotions come home tired at the end of the day. But is this tiredness only because they have worked hard, or might it also be related to their inability to be vulnerable with their wives? More often than not the answer is the latter. Not that their work isn't a drain on their energy—it is. But when they also hold their feelings back, they may use up any reserves of energy that might have gone into their relationships. Instead of talking to their wives and sharing life experiences, they sit in front of the television and become very boring people.

Another problem that can grow from the good husband's fear of being vulnerable is alcoholism and/or drug abuse. Whether he prefers a couple of martinis, a six pack of beer, or a joint when he comes home from work, the motive is the same: escape from the anxiety, resentment, frustration, and pressure he may be experiencing. He doesn't intend to get drunk or stoned—he just wants to "take the edge off." He wants to relax. The problem is that alcohol and drugs really do take the edge off. A person becomes increasingly dependent on these anesthetizing substances as his or her feelings of conflict go unresolved—and they go unresolved, in part, because that individual *thinks* he or she has found an effective way of making them disappear. In time, the drinking or the use of drugs can become a habit, developing into a physical need as the body chemistry adjusts to build a tolerance of these foreign substances.

When the good husband anesthetizes himself, he creates a psychological barrier between himself and his wife. He may start out consuming only small amounts of alcohol or drugs, but after a while a personality change occurs that makes meaningful communications between him and his wife impossible. In counseling, many wives complain about being "turned off" by their husbands after a few drinks. These wives are not turned off because their husbands are getting drunk (which they usually aren't doing), but by something the drinking represents to them. Usually it represents personal rejection—the good husband cutting his wife off from his emotional life—and that is what hurts. The use of alcohol and drugs is a blatant emotional wall, something that seems even more threatening to the wife than her husband's refusal to communicate verbally or to allow himself to be vulnerable. The wife becomes acutely aware that she is being left out of her husband's emotional life. In addition, she may lose respect for her husband, believing that he is not facing up to his feelings or is using a crutch to escape from them.

Invulnerability, the basic plan for becoming a man in our culture, is a blueprint for self-destruction. It is so deeply embedded in the male consciousness, however, that becoming aware of it and admitting to its dead ends, is a truly momentous task, one that men don't take lightly. Many experts observe that, indeed, living up to the masculine ideal often overshadows the instinct to survive.

The good husband's inability to be vulnerable kills or handicaps his ability to form any intimate relationship, particularly with his wife. As a result, he has no real place to be himself. He feels compelled to keep up his wall, so that no one really knows him, and he thus becomes the architect of his own loneliness and alienation. He doesn't want to become aware of himself. It's too threatening, and so he seeks a place to hide. As Sidney Jourad states in his book, *Transparent Self*, "If a man is reluctant to make himself known to another person, even to his spouse, because it is not manly, thus to be psychologically naked, then it follows that men will be difficult to love. That is, it will be difficult for a woman or another man to know the immediate present state of man's self, and his needs will thereby go unmet. Some men are so skilled at dissembling, at 'seeming,' that even their wives will not know when they are lonely, anxious, or hungering for affection. And the men, blocked by pride, dare not disclose their despair or need."

Some men run from their feelings by keeping busy all the time. Such a man has a hard time relaxing and "doing nothing." To not have a project or goal would mean that he would have to sit still. Then he might start to think and become aware of his feelings, and that's too uncomfortable.

One of the good husband's favorite ways of escaping from himself, and from being intimate with his wife, is watching television. How many wives in America want to blow up their television sets because they feel that they are in competition with them for their husbands' attention? In the United States, television is truly the opiate of marriage, but it is especially the opiate for the good husband.

Eventually, the good husband may be forced to look at himself and the emotional vacuum that he has created for himself. But all too often, he has to be "up against the wall" before he does anything about it. When his wife leaves him, or when he finds out that she is having an affair with another man or has filed for divorce, he wakes up. For some men, just having their wives go back to school or work, or show any interest in becoming more independent, can threaten them enough to shake them awake.

Once the good husband's barrier to being vulnerable starts to break down, he has a chance for real growth and change. Usually though, this change begins with depression, insecurity, and wild accusations. He may blame his wife for rocking the boat. He thinks he is no longer *a man* when he becomes vulnerable, and he has no cultural support system to tell him otherwise. It is no wonder that he panics and sometimes resorts to juvenile behavior before he finally grows up and begins to enjoy his newly found life.

Wives Who Never Go All the Way

The good wife, and women in general, also have a hard time being vulnerable in certain areas. Many of the things that happen to men as a result of not being vulnerable can happen to women as well. Unlike men, women have been given permission to feel and to express their feelings. However, that doesn't mean they will always feel free to express feelings. They may have grown up in families where the expression of certain emotions was taboo, and they are thus confused about what is acceptable and what is not acceptable to express. One major difference between men and women is that the woman will not feel that she is less of a woman if she cries or becomes emotional, whereas a man might question his masculinity under the same circumstances.

Two areas in which married women have a hard time being
vulnerable are: (1) expressing their emotions of anger and resentment in a clear, constructive manner, and (2) asking clearly for
what they want from their husbands. A woman who expresses any
dissatisfaction at all in her husband is behaving in a manner that
is not sanctioned by our culture, and therefore she is exposed to
the criticism and judgment of others. This is the source of much
potential pain for her.

In my work with couples, I find it generally true that women
have a more difficult time than men expressing their anger. The
stereotype in our culture is that "good girls never get angry." Anger isn't nice and ladylike. They are taught to hold their anger in,
repress it, and smile. Where does the anger go? Well, it goes "out
the back door," a phenomenon that I will explain shortly.

Many of you are probably saying, "I know lots of women who
get angry." That's true. But how do they express their anger? Do
they choose a clear, responsible form of communication? Many
times they do not. Their anger goes "out the back door" and generally gets expressed indirectly through yelling, sarcasm, moodi-
ness, crying and being extremely critical. These forms of communication may seem to be the only forms of expression open to her
because she would not be a "good girl" if she expressed herself
more directly.

The woman who follows the good-wife fantasy has a difficult
time being responsible for herself and communicating her needs
clearly. She has been taught to please everyone before she demands anything for herself. Please your kids, your husband, your
parents and friends—but remember, good wife, you're taking a
big risk if you ask that your own needs be recognized. The good
wife risks being judged by others, of course, but she also risks
being judged by herself, by that part deep inside her that says she
is breaking the rules, not living up to her parents' and her society's
expectations. The judgment that comes from within might say
something like, "Don't be so selfish, self-centered, demanding,
aggressive, bitchy, dominating, castrating." To express her honest
needs or wants, she must become fully aware of her good-wife
fantasies and recognize this new priority in her life: allowing herself to become vulnerable.

Vulnerability and Sex

Vulnerability plays a major role in the enjoyment of a longer term sexual relationship in marriage. I find that I am most vulnerable when I'm not exercising conscious control over myself—for example, when I've had too much to drink, or if I were to find that the brakes had suddenly failed on my car. The actions of beginning snow skiers show what it is like to feel out of control. As they race down the slope, they are fighting for control, and they ski tight and stiff. They get worn out just fighting the pull of gravity down the mountain. The reason for this is that they are afraid to let go, to relinquish their fight for control. They are afraid they won't be able to regain control in case something happens. They think they won't be able to stop. Experienced snow skiers, on the other hand, ski loose and free, submitting gracefully to the pull of the mountain. They can let go of that fight for control because they have the confidence that they can regain control at any time. This analogy helps illustrate an important point: pleasure and personal satisfaction increase as you become confident enough in your own skills to relinquish control. Letting go is allowing yourself to be vulnerable.

Letting go physically as well as mentally, especially in the context of a sexual relationship, leads to the experience of enjoying orgasm. During orgasm, a person relinquishes control involuntarily. It is virtually impossible to have an orgasm on demand. To enjoy sex, one must be able to abandon oneself to the erotic experience. One must be able, at least temporarily, to give up control and contact with the environment.

What happens if a person doesn't let go or become vulnerable outside the bedroom or in the nonsexual physical areas of their relationship? They probably will not completely let go during sex either. They may interact sexually. They may even have an orgasm. However, the intensity of the experience may be significantly dulled. Under these circumstances, the sexual experience becomes boring and dull.

It's also true that a person can have an exciting, intense sexual experience with another person and yet have little or no sense of being vulnerable—especially in the very early part of a relationship or with a "one-night stand." It is possible to have this type of sexual experience because the newness or novelty of the situation, the adventure of it, makes it exciting. But in addition—and this is important—there isn't a great deal of built-up resentment to get in the way of experiencing sexual feelings.

Over a period of time, the feelings of excitement that grow out of the novelty and newness of the situation start to fade. Also, because we get quickly caught up in the roles of the marriage fantasy, feelings of resentment or anger may start to develop. At the point when resentment begins to build, there's an important choice to be made. You can open up emotionally and become vulnerable, or you can leave that person and move on to a new relationship, repeating the pattern all over again. To have a long-term relationship with an enjoyable and intense sexual ingredient, it is essential that both people become vulnerable, preferably in *all* areas of their relationship.

Vulnerability is the cornerstone of a good marriage. Without it, a couple is doomed to a relationship that may be functional, but dull. Marriage partners who don't share their vulnerabilities don't express what they really feel inside, and they have trouble just being themselves. We live in a world that discourages the true expression of self. But in our own homes, we can build a refuge where we can let go and be human. Through the process of learning to let ourselves be vulnerable to those we love, we come to know ourselves. As we get to know ourselves, we are able to grow and make changes. Without this important process available within the institution of marriage, a person falls into static life patterns and his or her life becomes habitual, unexciting, and empty.

Part II
Working It Out:
The Tools for Change

In the first part of this book, we explored some of the common problems that arise in marriage. In this part, we will consider some solutions to the problems. I call this section "Tools for Change" because it contains descriptions of specific skills you can incorporate into your life. I like the term *tools* as a label because, just as learning the mental tools of mathematics and design allow an architect to build a desired structure, so can the tools introduced here help you and your spouse to build the kind of marriage relationship you desire.

7. Neutrality: A Key to Implementing Change

After a few years of marriage, a husband and wife become so familiar with each other's patterns of behavior that they can usually predict what the other's response will be in any given circumstances. As one man told me during a counseling session, "My wife knows what I'm going to to before I know what I'm going to do myself." Although there are advantages to knowing another person this well, there are also disadvantages, and the chief disadvantage is that such knowledge can inhibit change, even change that is desired by both partners in a marriage.

In order to understand how knowledge of a mate's behavior patterns can handicap that person's movement toward change, we have only to look at a few of the phrases that commonly come up in domestic arguments. For example, a wife may say to her husband, "You *always* do it that way." Or a husband may say to his wife, "*Every time* we talk, you clam up and sulk." While such observations may be accurate, they put people on the defensive, frequently causing them to "dig in their heels" and stay the way they are instead of encouraging the changes both partners desire.

Not only do we define and limit our partner's behavior through the attitudes expressed in these phrases, we also limit ourselves. We've all heard the phrase, "That's the way I am and I can't change it" more times than we can count. The belief expressed in this phrase is one of the most common misconceptions about human nature. Although we are born with a certain eye color or hair color, we are *not* born with certain attitudes or behavior patterns. Rather, we learn the ways we behave, and because our behavior patterns *are* learned ways we are not stuck with them. If you are motivated to change, you can learn new patterns of behavior, just as you learned the old ones, and the fact that you can do this is what gives you control of your life.

When marriage partners are repeatedly reminded of their habits of behavior in the past, they feel less motivated to change. Such criticism for past behavior is a type of mental sabotage. Often a husband or wife dwells on the past to prove who was right or wrong back then—in short, to place blame. It is important to understand your past so that you can improve your future, but many couples I see use the past as an emotional sledgehammer to drive their mates into the ground. This process is different from when one partner asks the other to acknowledge how he or she felt about some past incident, for even after feelings have been acknowledged, the partner keeps bringing up the past. People hammer away at past incidents for many reasons, but the most common ones are to punish a spouse for an old or even imagined abuse, or to keep emotional distance between them, as a way of preventing possible future hurt. In the latter case, the timing of the communication about the past is crucial: it seems that just as the couple is starting to feel close again, the scarred partner brings up another old incident and creates a new barrier between them.

Similar to the partner who dwells on the past is the one who is anxious about the future. These people are concerned about the what if's of their relationships. They ask questions like, "What if he doesn't talk to me?" and "What if this therapy doesn't work?" Again, such people are not focusing on the present. In their minds, at least, they live in the future, always putting mental or emotional distance between themselves and their partner. The sad thing is that their thoughts about the future tend to control their emotions, making their worst dreams come true. This is what is often known as the "self-fulfilling prophecy" pattern.

The concept of *neutrality* helps us to focus on the here and now. What is going on between you and your spouse right now? What is working to bring you closer, and what are you and your spouse doing to keep distance between you? The past cannot be changed, and the future cannot be seen. One's relationship with another person can only be enjoyed in the present.

Encouraging neutrality and keeping focused on the present allow room for the expression of new and different attitudes and behaviors. The related concept of *perception validity* supports the view that differences between partners in a relationship are "good." Different points of view can add flexibility and variety to a relationship, making the time these people spend together more interesting and exciting. The word *perception*, in this context, refers to the way people interpret their experiences through their own senses as well as in the light of their unique past experiences.

Perception Validity: Learning to Love the Differences

Let us imagine that three people are standing at an intersection when suddenly there's a traffic accident. All three people witness the accident, but when the police question them, they get three slightly different stories. The police want to know which one of these three views is the *right* view of how this accident occurred. However, notwithstanding a court of law, all three views or perceptions are *right*, even though they are *different*.

In my practice, I often hear husbands and wives struggling to establish whose view was right and whose was wrong. Their arguments often go something like this:

"Why didn't you put gas in the car?"

"You said you were going to do it."

"I didn't say that. I asked you to do it."

"You did no such thing. If you'd asked me, I would have done it."

Or:

"Every time we go out to dinner, you don't like the food."

"You're wrong. I do like the food. It's just the restaurants you pick that I don't like."

Judging by the vehemence with which many couples argue—even over trivialities—one might think they were arguing over whose religion was "right." Is Buddha right, or Mohammad, or Jesus—or all religions and gods false? Trying to prove the validity of one's individual view of the world is a futile effort, whether the discussion concerns one's religious beliefs or one's preferences in food. Furthermore, among couples, it is common for one partner or the other to attempt to validate his or her own point of view by proving how "wrong" his or her mate is.

When I worked with schizophrenic teenagers at a state psychiatric hospital, one boy who was a patient there gave me an unforgettable lesson in the concept of perception validity. His name was Harry. Nearly every night, Harry would act as if his father was coming after him with an axe. Harry so believed in his fantasy that he'd become hysterical and try to run away. In an effort to assuage his fears, I would tell him that his father wasn't really coming after him, that his father lived a long way from the hospital. I argued with Harry and told him that there was *no reason* for him to be afraid. But what I was saying to him, in essence, was that his feelings and perceptions had no logical grounds, and he should stop acting crazy. So when I communicated with Harry in this manner, it was like talking to a wall—he did not even acknowledge my existence. I was fresh out of college with my B.A. in psychology, and I thought I knew exactly what I was doing. I didn't.

Frustrated with my efforts to reason with Harry, I finally tried something different. He started into one of his usual episodes, and I told him, "Yes, Harry, I can see you're afraid that your father is coming after you with an axe." He turned to me and said, "Dan, what should I do? Where can I hide?" For the first time in our relationship, *I acknowledged Harry's perception of reality*—and for the first time, he acknowledged my existence and communicated with me. Even though I believed Harry's perceptions were crazy, I accepted the fact that they were real and made complete sense to Harry. I wasn't able to communicate about our *differences* of perception until I had first accepted the validity of Harry's perceptions.

Though the example of Harry is a bizarre one, the same mechanisms are at work in most of the arguments we have in marriage. Arguing over right or wrong, true or false, may be intellectually stimulating. But if a couple argues the validity of what they feel emotionally, or what they perceive, one or both partners can end up hurting each other's feelings, creating an atmosphere of distrust and fear that inhibits honest and open communication.

When that happens, the intimacy between them breaks down and they feel distant or even lonely.

Some people find it very difficult to accept differences of perception or opinion in the people close to them. If someone disagrees with them, they question the validity of their own perceptions and feel insecure about their own viewpoints. Instead of accepting the possibility that there can be different points of view and that all these points of view can be right, the insecure person wants to change, convince, pressure, or convert the other person to his or her own perception. Once the conversion is made, the insecure person feels more comfortable, because no one is threatening his or her special view of the world.

In all relationships, but especially in marriage, it is important to accept the fact that each of us sees the world in a slightly different way. That is what makes each person unique. Accepting the fact of being different allows us to love those who are not like ourselves. When two people can learn to live with each other's differences and validate them, rather than trying to win them over or negate them, both individuals are richer for the experience.

8. *Intimate Communications: Letting Your Mate Know Who You Are*

As a marriage counselor, I'm in the business of helping people to improve their relationships with their mates. But just passing out psychological theory does not produce much change, I've found. Real change occurs only when people learn specific ways to integrate the concepts I discuss with them into their day-to-day experiences with their marriage partners.

Intimate communication is the term I use to describe what husbands and wives do when they tell each other about themselves—about their deepest emotions, their fears, and their most personal wants or needs. Many people come into counseling believing that they communicate well, but most of them say they don't. And even many of those who believe that they communicate well discover that their communications are not, in the final analysis, either personal or intimate. They have good conversations, and they have intellectual discussions about their kids, their parents, their friends, or the political scene. But problems arise for them when they start talking about themselves. In the beginning of their relationships, these people may have been able to communicate intimately with their partners, expressing their feelings and personal secrets, their dreams and aspirations. But somewhere in the course of their marriage, perhaps as they had to confront the various personal conflicts normal to marriage, their intimate communication system broke down. As a result, they began to avoid personal subjects and talk about things outside of the intimate sphere.

Nowhere in our culture are we taught how to communicate intimately. Most people of our parents' generation talked together only when they were outside the range of their children's hearing. Or they yelled at each other. So a newly married couple often has little or no experience in effective and intimate communication. They certainly didn't have a class on communication in high school or college. Somehow we've all gotten the idea that if two people are in love, they will just naturally get along well with each other. "Why should you have to teach marriage partners how to talk to each other? They can work it out on their own. They don't need any help," the popular myth seems to say.

The communication of emotions is the primary way we let ourselves be vulnerable to our mates. The way an emotion is communicated and the degree to which it is expressed by a couple generally shows how vulnerable and intimate two people are with each other. But people are generally not comfortable with intimate communication. For example, what would probably happen if someone asked me how I was doing, and I replied, "I'm feeling lonely and afraid"? Most likely, the person who had asked how I was would be so surprised he or she wouldn't know what to say. This would not necessarily mean that person was uncaring or indifferent to my feelings, but he or she is probably not accustomed to that level of intimacy in everyday communication. To be sure, I'm not advocating that people open themselves up to the point that they tell everyone they meet how they're really feeling. Most of the time social cordialities, though superficial, serve our needs very well. But in marriage, where feelings are so important, intimate communication is essential.

Acting Out Emotions

Often people try to communicate their feelings nonverbally. Examples of nonverbal communication are when a person slams a door, or mopes around the house, or paces back and forth, or sits in a chair and sighs a lot. This person is trying to communicate his or her emotions through behavior, through sounds and body language.

How do you know, for certain, what people are thinking or feeling when they express themselves in these ways? The truth is that it is impossible to know exactly what another person is feeling unless he or she tells you. When your spouse slams a door and sits down in a chair with his or her back to you, refusing to speak, it would be reasonable to assume that he or she is angry, frustrated, or hurt. I use the word *assume* advisedly, because in nonverbal communication, the would-be listener must interpret the other person's behavior—and this can lead to real trouble.

Let us say that a husband assumes his wife is angry with him because she is acting grumpy and doesn't want to talk to him. Rather than deal with the matter now, he decides to leave her alone until she feels better. After leaving her alone all day, he discovers that she wasn't angry with him at all. Instead, she was angry at a friend of hers. But now she is mad at him, too, because he seemed indifferent to her troubles. When you act as if your assumptions are facts, you set yourself up to be an ass or a fool. An easy way to remember this concept is to take apart the word *assume* and see what it stands for: ASS-U-ME—that is, an ass out of you and me.

There's nothing wrong with two partners making assumptions during the *process* of intimate communication. You might guess at what's troubling your spouse and then ask if that's what he or she is feeling. But to avoid making an "ass" of yourself, you must check out the validity of your assumption with the person about whom you are making that assumption. For example:

"I have the feeling that you are angry with me. Is that true?"

"No, I'm not angry with you, I'm just feeling hurt and disappointed that my mother didn't call." Or the same person might have said, "Yes, I'm angry with you for leaving the house in such a mess."

In the first response, the assumption turned out to be false or invalid, so it should be thrown out. However, the second response indicates that the assumption is valid, and there is no misunderstanding. Assumptions in communication become a problem only when they are acted on automatically as if they were facts.

People who act out their emotions rather than communicating them verbally not only leave their communications open to wrong assumptions, but also prevent intimacy from developing in their relationships. When people act out their emotions, they are not being vulnerable or open to their spouses. How can they be vulnerable if they haven't opened up and taken the risk necessary to verbalize their emotions for their spouses to hear? To put it mildly, it is hard to be intimate with someone who is just sitting in a chair and *acting* angry or sad, but not saying a word.

Dumping Emotions

Another way people project emotion without communicating is through a verbal style called "dumping." Although words are involved, dumping prevents intimacy just as acting out in the nonverbal style does. It goes something like this:

"John, how many times have I told you not to leave your clothes all over the place? You really shouldn't do that because you set such a poor example for the kids. You are so sloppy. I don't know how I live with you. I'm always having to tell you about it, and you never seem to understand. Please listen to me. I'm just trying to be honest with you and tell you how I feel."

Most likely this woman is feeling hurt, angry, maybe even frustrated, but we can only *assume* that these are her feelings. There is no way to tell, from what she said, how she is actually feeling. However, had you been on the receiving end of the above monologue, you would probably feel angry or hurt. Few adults like to be talked to in this manner, especially not by someone they love.

How do people on the receiving end express their feelings of hurt and anger? Usually they take one of two paths. They may react defensively with anger and aggression. For example, John might say to his wife, "You are not so neat yourself. You leave clothes all over the place, too. So who are you to judge?" The person on the receiving end of this response will probably become defensive, too, and launch a counterattack. Generally, this form of communication—attack/defend—escalates in volume and intensity until neither one can hear what the other is saying. Then they usually reach a certain point of frustration, quit yelling, and finally fall into sulking. Nothing is resolved. Neither of them has been able to communicate their feelings, and now both of them feel miserable. Have they become closer or more intimate? On the contrary, the gap between them has probably been widened. Some couples take hours to cool off after such encounters, some take days, and often there are residual feelings of anger, frustration, or pain that inhibit intimacy for months.

A second common way that people respond after receiving such

an attack is by withdrawing completely from the interaction.
They may just "clam up" or they may literally "stalk off" to get
away from the situation. Whatever path of withdrawal the person
takes, the message is the same: "I'm not listening to you when you
talk like that!" The person who launched the original attack then
becomes increasingly angry because his or her emotions are not
being acknowledged, and because the person with whom they
wished to communicate obviously isn't listening. Both partners
end up feeling ignored and hurt, often unaware of the mechanism
that precipitated their alienation from one another.

You Messages: Creating an Adversary

Sentences that begin with the word *you* should tip a person off to
the fact that he or she is being *dumped* on. For example, phrases
such as "you should," or "you always," or "you never, you dum-
my," or any variation on this theme are *you* messages. Go back to
the communication given earlier about the sloppy husband and
see how many *you* messages there are. The entire example is a
series of *you* messages. Many books that deal with parent-child
communication talk about *you* messages as being a poor form of
communication even when talking to children. Believe me, they
are just as ineffective with adults.

The reason that *you* messages are not effective is that the people
using them are not disclosing any of their emotions. They are not
taking responsibility for their feelings. They are unable to express
what it is that they feel. Instead, they "dump" their emotions in a
barrage of accusations, orders, complaints, and judgments. The
person who communicates through the use of *you* messages tells
you all about yourself—what you should do, what you never do or
always do, but they don't tell you about themselves for that would
make them vulnerable.

I Messages: The Art of Intimate Verbalization

I messages are sentences that start with the pronoun *I*. Three types
of *I* messages are of particular importance to us here: "I feel," "I
want," and "I need." These are the key phrases in effective, intimate communication.

Using *I* messages, a person might say, "*I feel* angry when all these clothes are left on the floor," or "*I feel* disappointed and sad when you cancel out at the last minute," or "*I feel* excited when you invite me out to dinner," or "*I feel* hurt when you make cracks about the way I look." All these statements start with the phrase "I feel," followed by the words that describe your *emotion*. There can be variations, such as the addition of adverbs, or you might even leave out the word *feel* and just say, for example, "*I appreciate* it when you clean up after yourself."

When a husband communicates his emotions through *I* messages, he is opening up and becoming vulnerable. He is taking responsibility for how he feels by telling exactly the emotions he is feeling. His wife needn't *assume* how her husband feels because he has told her what he feels. He is giving her intimate information about himself, information that he probably doesn't share with many people. He is giving her a chance to know him in an intimate way—but he is also taking a risk. The feelings he makes known might be judged by her, or she might reject him when she learns about his feelings, and this, obviously, could hurt. This is the basic fear of becoming vulnerable. An example of a rejection response to an *I* message might be the following exchange between a husband and his wife.

"I'm feeling really afraid of going to that party tonight, honey."

"Well, you shouldn't be afraid. You're just acting silly. So get dressed and let's go!" If the husband who is afraid of going to the party gets this kind of response, he might not only feel afraid, he may also feel *hurt*. Following the hurt may come anger at being judged and put down about the way he feels. He will probably either become defensive or withdraw into silence from the interaction.

The fear of being hurt is the main reason people avoid putting themselves in a vulnerable position. The problem with people letting this fear run their lives is that it prevents their enjoying intimacy with their mates. Their relationships remain superficial. However, when they choose to take a risk and become vulnerable, then they are giving their relationships a chance to become close and intimate. If a person continually gets hurt, then he or she may

want to reconsider seriously whether or not he or she wants to
stay in the relationship, or, at least, stay in it in any intimate way.
When a spouse becomes vulnerable in a marriage, the worst that
can happen is that he or she may find that intimacy has no chance.
On the other hand, if neither partner takes the risk in becoming
vulnerable, intimacy may never become possible.

Sometimes people misunderstand how to use *I* messages. Here
are some examples you should try to avoid: "I just want to be open
and honest with you and tell you how I feel. I really feel you are
inconsiderate of me and my feelings," or "I feel you should go to
the store," or "I feel like the rules should change," or "I feel that
you should call me when you go out." A close examination of
these statements quickly reveals that they are not true *I* messages,
but only sentences onto which the phrase, "I feel," has been
tacked. In reality, they are *you* messages. Remember, an *I* message
describes a feeling experienced by the speaker. Have you ever
experienced the emotions "you," or "that," or "like?" Of course not.
What the person in the first example is saying is, "I think you are
inconsiderate of me." This person may—in fact, probably does—
feel something (angry, sad, etc.) about the behavior he or she may
feel shows inconsideration, but has not said yet how he or she
feels. Expressing what they think, rather than what they feel, is a
common way that people hide their emotions from their partners.
It is a lot safer, emotionally, to stay "in your head" than to express
the emotions that involve your entire being.

Another valuable *I* message for building intimate communication begins with the phrase, "I want." But what were most of us
taught about stating what we wanted as children? Most people
were told again and again how *selfish* they were when they asked
for things for themselves. In essence, we were taught not to talk
about what we *want*. Younger children who have not yet learned
this lesson have no trouble taking responsibility for what they
want. They will tell their parents, "I want an ice cream cone," or "I
want to go home," or "I want to go outside." Their parents don't
have to guess or make assumptions—the children themselves are
very clear about what they want. If there is a problem in this, it is
not in the asking but in the *expectation*; children fully expect to get

what they want simply because they've asked for it. And when they don't get what they want they may feel angry or hurt, unable to understand why anything must stand in the way of their complete satisfaction.

What I am suggesting is that you express what you want in the same clear, direct manner you used as a child, but without the hook that most children put at the end—that is, without the expectation that just because you ask for something, you are going to get it. That expectation is selfish, aggressive, demanding, and inconsiderate of the wants or needs of the person you love. Expressing what you want in an intimate relationship without selfish expectation is a responsible way of taking care of yourself. You assert your wants *in hopes* that you will get them, putting them out on the table for negotiation.

In my work, I have heard people argue against communicating what they want in the clear, direct ways I advise. The argument is a common one that is based on myths embedded in our society's marriage fantasy. The argument runs something like this: "If I have to tell you what I want, then it just isn't worth it! If you don't know by now what I want, then who have you been living with anyway? Besides, if I tell you what I want, then you are just doing it because I asked. I want you to do things for me without me having to ask." This myth would work if we were all psychics with powerful abilities to read minds—but we are obviously not. People who insist that their partners develop mind-reading skills generally end up feeling misunderstood, frustrated, and hurt. They don't get what they want. They only get what their partners *assume*— there's that word again—they want.

If a person has expressed clearly what he or she wants, and that person's partner agrees to give what is asked for, then there should be no need for the want to be expressed over and over again. If he or she must keep asking for what he or she wants, then either that person's partner didn't understand the request or there is some other emotional problem that needs to be solved in this relationship.

Many married people are afraid to express what they want because they fear conflict. No matter how much they're in love,

people are never carbon copies of each other. Because they are
different, they are not always going to want the same things their
partners want. For example, one may want to go out to dinner,
while the other wants to eat at home. One may want to make love,
while the other wants to go to sleep. Conflicts of this kind are
normal in marriage, and learning to deal effectively with this fact
can be as rewarding as it is difficult. One common but destructive
belief is the notion that a couple that does not have conflicts has a
good marriage. The truth of the matter is that I have seen hundreds of these couples, all of them seeking solutions to their "in-
visible" problems.

What I have learned is that the classic, smoothly running marriage—the "model" marriage—usually involves two very insecure people. All too often, one discovers in such marriages a man
and a woman who are afraid of confrontation and their own feelings of anger. When potential conflicts arise between them, one or
both may avoid the situation by "selling themselves out" and de-
ferring to the other's wants rather than expressing their own
wants. They are seldom aware that, in the long run, they are setting up their marriage for failure. Here's an example of an exchange between the two partners in such a marriage:

"What do you want to do tonight, dear?"

"Oh, whatever you want to do."

"Well, I want to do whatever you want to do!"

Here is a case where neither husband nor wife wants to take
responsibility for what they want. Another exchange might run as
follows: He says, "I want to go to the football game this weekend,"
and even though his wife hates football, she says, "Oh, sure, that
sounds great. Whatever *you* would like, honey." This wife is "selling out." What does *she* really want? Perhaps she is hiding the fact
that she wants to go to Carmel for the weekend. Only she doesn't
express this want because she prefers to avoid a fight.

This lack of assertiveness is a major problem in many marriages.
When people give in, when they try to be *nice* in an intimate
relationship and don't tell each other what they really want,
they're ultimately hurting themselves as well as the relationship.
If they don't express what they want, they are not going to get it.

And after a period of not getting what they want, they are going to feel hurt and resentful toward their spouses. This is the point when people begin to resent being married. For the moment, it may seem very nice to be living together without conflict or hassle, but in the long run, when one or both partners begin to cash in on their past-due resentments, the emotional price tag for all this "niceness" is revealed.

Everything described thus far has been based on the assumption that both people in the marriage have things they want. But what if they don't want anything? Or what if they really have no preference? Then none of this applies. Resentment will not develop because the person with no preferences is not selling out.

Even if both people in a relationship express what they want, they may still have difficulty communicating their wants clearly. Many people express their wants in such vague, nebulous ways that only they themselves can understand what they want. Examples of this type of "I want" statement are: "I want you to be more romantic"; "I want to be understood"; "I want respect"; "I want more love." All these *I* messages sound good, but they are all much too broad, far too open to interpretation. The last of these example statements may be stereotypical, but it serves to illustrate a good point. The wife says to her husband, "I want more love. I don't feel you really care for me." The husband replies, "Here's my paycheck. Go buy yourself some new clothes." His wife retorts, "That's not what I want. I want you to love me." The husband reacts defensively: "Look, I worked hard to get you this big house and that swimming pool and your new car. If that's not love, then I don't know what you want." In a way, he's telling the truth: he really *doesn't* know what she wants. And there is no way for him to know unless she tells him *exactly* what he can do to demonstrate his love. He thinks he is expressing his love by giving her things. She doesn't see it that way, because, to her, love is expressed in another way. It is as if they're using two different languages, each foreign to the other. The longer they communicate, the more frustrated, hurt, and disappointed both people become. They may decide not to express what they want at all, because "It's just not worth it."

Another example of the same problem, but one with some possibility for resolution of the frustration, occurred during a marriage counseling session I had with a young couple. It went like this: The husband said to his wife, "I want you to show me more respect." I interrupted and said, "What's one thing she could *do* that would show you her respect?" He turned to her and replied, "Stop putting me down in front of our children." The message was clear. The wife now had a specific line of action to take. In his first rather unclear request, the husband left much to the imagination. In the second request, there could be no room for assumption. His wife had been asked to show respect, and now she knew one sure way to show it.

When you express what you want, "paint a picture" so that the person who is in a position to fill that need can see exactly what you want. You greatly increase your chances of getting what you want when your *I* message is clear and specific. An "I want" message is like a verbal prescription for curing the *ill* that's troubling you. Many people communicate what they don't like about their partner's behavior, but seldom do they express what they *want*— that is, they never tell their spouses how to improve the situation. You are letting yourself be vulnerable to your partner when you allow him or her to understand what you want from the relationship and from life in general.

I Need Is Different Than *I Want*

We should draw a distinction here between *wants* and *needs*. Needs are trust, sex, respect, companionship, and intimate communication. The difference between needs and wants is that *needs* are not negotiable. They have to be met. *Wants*, however, are negotiable. What *I need* never changes, but what *I want* may change from moment to moment.

The statement is often made, particularly in reference to marriage, that one person cannot meet all the needs of another person. This statement is true—but only up to a point. What it fails to mention is what *types* of needs are being discussed. People have certain core or "universal" needs that have to be met. Such needs are prerequisites for the continuance of any loving relationship.

People generally feel resentment and pain when even one of these needs goes unmet, even for a relatively short period of time. But needs differ. One person may have a long list of needs, whereas another may have only one need—for example, emotional or financial security. That one need may suffice for that person, even when no other needs are being met.

Sometimes needs can, or even *must*, be met by someone outside the marriage. For example, in my own case, I need physical activities and certain intellectual pursuits. I have a need for tennis or skiing, but my wife doesn't have to participate in these activities in order for us to stay together. I go to professional workshops and programs to satisfy my need to stay intellectually stimulated in my field, but I don't need my wife to do these things with me. I can get these needs met with a friend or a colleague. It would be *nice* if she sometimes did these things with me, but it isn't necessary that she participate in these activities to make me happy with our marriage.

When people are unclear about their needs, I advise them to ask themselves this question, "If I were single again tomorrow, what would be my personal needs from an emotional point of view?" Once people become clear about their specific needs, their next step must be to communicate these needs and the ways in which they can be satisfied by their spouses.

Exercise No. 2: *I* Messages

PURPOSE: To develop skills expressing and listening to *I* messages.

PREPARATION: Make room for one hour of uninterrupted time with your mate.

EXERCISE: Sit facing each other. You will be taking turns expressing and listening. When you are the listener, do not interrupt your mate except to ask for clarification. While doing this exercise, do not argue, debate, or discuss any of the issues being raised. Listen as though you were an objective third person and did not have to do anything about the information you are receiving.

When you are the speaker, begin each of your statements with the pronoun *I* and express each of the following points to your mate:

1) *Appreciation:* Tell your mate one thing that you appreciate about him or her. Focus on a single feature of your mate's personality or behavior. It can be a small thing or a large one—that doesn't matter as much as being clear about what you feel and expressing your feelings in the *I* context.

2) *Resentment:* Tell your mate about one thing in his or her behavior that you resent. Be specific. Be clear. Be brief and focus on a single source of resentment. Begin each statement you make with the pronoun *I*.

3) *Want or Need:* Tell your mate about one thing you want or need from him or her. Describe a single specific action that he or she might take to satisfy this want or need.

Now reverse roles so that the listener becomes the speaker and the speaker becomes the listener.

You may repeat this exercise as many times as you wish, trading roles back and forth until one of you wants to stop.

After both partners have completed this exercise, do not further discuss the issues raised here. Although you may have strong feelings about some of the information communicated, bear in mind that you are not *required* to do anything about it, nor should you expect an immediate change in your mate's behavior because of what you have expressed here. You are not being ordered to change, in the way that your parents or teachers may have done when you were a child, nor are you assuming a parental role and ordering your spouse to change. Instead, you are exchanging information about what you and your mate feel you want from each other. What you finally choose to do with this information is entirely up to you.

Remember that asking does not guarantee that you will get what you want. Asking only *informs* the other person of your wants. Similarly, when others inform you of what they want, you are not obligated to fulfill their wants. There are no guarantees here.

9. Intimate Listening: Developing Your Third Ear

While it is important for a husband and wife to learn how to communicate with *I* messages, it is equally important that they learn how to listen to one another. After all, until a mesage is heard, no communication can occur.

Good listening in an intimate relationship must be learned. It is not something that comes naturally, although most people seem to think it should. As with learning how to hit a good backhand in tennis, once the skill is understood intellectually, it needs to be practiced until it requires little conscious thinking. Only at that point does it come naturally.

Ineffective Styles of Listening

For a moment, let us explore some common *ineffective* ways to listen. When I ask people how they listen, the most common answer I get is that they listen by being silent and maintaining direct eye contact. Of course, this is how we were taught to listen as children. As children, most of us were told by our parents again and again, "Be quiet and listen to what I'm going to tell you."

Now you might ask, "What's wrong with listening quietly and not interrupting the speaker?" The answer is simple. If a person is listening quietly to what you are saying, how do you know that he or she is understanding you? There is no way to tell. Eye contact doesn't help much. It is what is going on in a person's mind that is important. In counseling teenagers, for example, counselors learn that these young people are often very good at appearing to listen when they're not. They have learned that they don't need to listen as long as they appear to be doing so.

Good listeners make it clear to the person speaking that they are listening. The speaker should not have to wonder if he or she is being heard—the good listener makes that obvious. And the person who sits quietly as you speak gives you little or no indication of how much or how little of what you are saying is being heard.

At the opposite end of the scale is the listener who asks a lot of questions. Such listeners, in many cases, may be asking questions in an effort to show that they are interested or concerned about what the speaker is telling them. They may also be trying to clarify what the speaker is saying. On the surface, this all seems good, but where emotions are concerned, this method of listening can be a disaster.

When a person is trying to express his or her feelings, questions are like hurdles, constantly tripping them up. Questions like "When, how, where, why did you do that?" are all secondary to the emotion the speaker is trying to communicate. When a person *listens* in this way, the speaker is usually thinking, "Will you shut up and listen to me!" In addition, questions direct the flow of communication, often in a direction that was not intended by the speaker. All too often, the speaker becomes defensive instead of talking about what he or she wanted to express in the first place.

Finally, there is an *ineffective* way of listening that I call the "hard-sell" style. Hard-sell-listeners seem to be trying to convince you of how hard they're listening and how well they understand what you're trying to say. But somehow you're not at all convinced. The hard-sell listener might respond to you with, "Wow, I really hear where you're coming from," or "I can relate to that!" or "I hear you. I really understand what you're saying." The hard-sell listener may not use those exact phrases or others like them, but instead may make sounds, such as, "Uh-huh," "Yeah," or "I see." Again, the speaker still doesn't know if the listener understands what he or she is saying because the words or sounds made could apply no matter what the speaker was saying.

Effective Listening

Having considered some listening styles that do not work, let us now take a look at some that do. Effective styles of listening have been given many names—*active* listening, *reflective* listening, and *nondirective* listening, to list a few of them. All of these styles have similar themes and vary most in their emphasis.

Consider how the following exchange between a husband and wife might demonstrate effective listening methods. The scene opens as John comes home from work to find his wife Linda upset because he has arrived late. Since he recognizes that she is upset, he takes responsibility as a listener and does his best to hear her out:

> Linda: Where have you been? Dinner is ruined! At least you could have called.
>
> John: I got caught in a meeting and didn't realize how late it was getting.
>
> Linda: You didn't realize!
>
> John: You're really angry with me because I'm late. [Starts listening.]
>
> Linda: Sure I'm angry! I worked hard at preparing this dinner for us.
>
> John: So you're feeling disappointed about this evening.
>
> Linda: No, I'm not feeling disappointed about the evening. It's just the dinner I'm disappointed about.
>
> John: You seem less angry with me now than you were.
>
> Linda: Well, I'm feeling concerned about this happening again, because I know you get very involved in your work.
>
> John: You mean you're worried that I'm going to continue to be absent-minded.
>
> Linda: I am worried, but I didn't say you're absent-minded. I just want you to call me if you know you're going to be late. Can you do that?
>
> John: Yes, I promise I'll call you next time.

In this exchange, John makes it clear that he is listening to Linda. But what was he doing to make that clear? He was giving back specific information that told her he recognized why she was angry, disappointed, and concerned. The final test of his effectiveness is that Linda felt that she had been heard and that her husband cared enough about what she had said to agree to do something to avoid upsetting her again.

When I want to really listen to someone, I focus all my attention on him or her. It is as if I turn a spotlight on the person talking, and I don't take that spotlight away until he or she is finished talking. I focus on all the clues this person gives me through body language, inflection or tone of voice, facial expressions, and, of course, the words. Also, I will consider how I myself might feel (not think) if I were in the same place as the speaker. With all this information, I then ask myself, "From what the speaker is telling me, what is he or she feeling (not thinking)?" After I decide what the speaker seems to be telling me, I formulate a statement that will tell that person what I've heard. Then I feed this statement back to the speaker so that he or she can judge whether or not I have understood correctly.

In the above scene, John used feedback statements when he said to Linda, "You're really angry with me," "So you're feeling disappointed," "You seem less angry," and "You're worried." To each statement, Linda replied yes, she felt that way, or no, she didn't feel that way. Such statements provide the structure for a system of checks and balances. Misunderstandings are cleared up almost immediately through this clarification process (see Figure 14).

A feedback statement may sound like a question, but it is actually a statement that has an implied question mark at the end, a question mark that does not interrupt the speaker's flow of feeling. Interruptive questions sound more like, "Do you feel sad about . . . ?" instead of "You feel sad about . . ." Interruptive questions take the spotlight away from the speaker and make that person feel that no one is interested in hearing what he or she has to say.

The ingredient that made Linda, in the example given above, feel heard was that she was able to hear her listener, John, *verbally acknowledge* what she was feeling. When a speaker's emotions are acknowledged in this way, that person doesn't have to raise his or her voice. People feel like yelling in an argument not because they think those listening to them are literally deaf, but because they feel their listeners are deaf to the emotions they are trying to convey. The speaker who gets confirmation that he or she has been

Figure 14

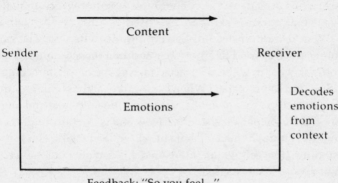

Feedback; "So you feel..."

heard stops yelling almost immediately. The situation is similar to what happens when we try to bury our emotions: emotions that aren't acknowledged don't go away, but knock louder and louder until they are acknowledged. Here, as we consider listening skills, we see that speakers will get louder and louder until they feel their emotions have been acknowledged.

A gentle warning, however. Effective listening is all to frequently misused—even by individuals who have the best of intentions. People read how to do it in a book and start applying it to every situation in life. They begin to sound like a broken record. They apply this style of listening even when there is no real need—for example, when not a great deal of emotion is being expressed or when there isn't any conflict. When this style of listening is used in the wrong situations, the listener begins to sound patronizing. So be thoughtful about using this skill. Like all good tools, it has its specific applications.

Exploring Pitfalls in Order to Avoid Them

The example I gave of John and Linda was an ideal exchange between husband and wife, but until two people have had a good deal of practice in communicating and listening to each other effectively, less effective exchanges will tend to dominate. Often, I've found, it helps couples to have an example to identify where

they are now, in order to plan better where they want to go. Therefore, let us consider some common scenarios in which noneffec-
tive communication skills are exercised.

What if John, instead of listening to his wife when he came
home late, had tried to ignore her and had turned on the television? Or, what if, when she started talking, he had clammed up or
hid behind a newspaper? When he does any of these things, Linda
feels he doesn't care about her feelings. She feels hurt and angry,
ignored by the person she loves. Now she is not only angry with
him for coming home late, but she is also upset with him for not
listening. Her feelings are intensified, instead of being reduced as
in our more ideal example.

Another path that John could have followed would have been
to get angry with her for being angry at him. Instead of listening,
he could have responded with comments that expressed his own
anger: "Don't bug me! I had a hard day," or "Don't make such a big
deal about your dinner. I'll take you out if it's ruined," or "You
don't always call *me* when *you* are late," or "Hey, I had a great day. I
come home and look how upset you make me. You should be glad
I come home at all with the way you treat me after I've worked so
hard at the office!" These are typical defensive *you* messages that
usually fan the flames of any emotional situation. John came
home emotionally upset. Linda didn't make him upset. The more
upset she becomes, the angrier John becomes until, finally, they
are yelling at one another. This situation may escalate until one of
them walks off in frustration or breaks down and starts to cry.
Intimacy between John and Linda disappears. They may not talk
to each other for a day or more, and the feelings of hurt and anger
increase during this time. The longer this period of silence continues, the more damage is done to the relationship.

Choosing to listen rather than to withdraw or defend oneself is
difficult. The temptation to do either or both of these is great—
even when both people know better. It takes restraint not to get
"sucked in" when responding to a partner who is upset. In my
own case, I know that when I let myself get sucked in and react by
withdrawing or being defensive, I lose some self-respect. For the
sake of my self-esteem, I prefer to listen effectively to my spouse.

When Reason Blocks Your Ears

Being logical or rational with someone who is being emotional is like trying to mix oil and water. It is ineffective at best. When a spouse is emotional, he or she is not going to be able to hear anything that is being said until the emotional level has lowered. For example, if a man comes in to see me for counseling after he discovers that his wife is having an affair with his best friend, he is going to be emotionally upset. It will be difficult for him to hear anything I have to say, but it will be doubly hard for him to hear me if I try to speak logically and rationally. The chances are that he will interrupt me to express all that he is feeling. So, in such a case, I would put the spotlight on him and let him express his emotions until he felt satisfied. Only after his emotions have been expressed and acknowledged will he be able to start listening and understanding what I might have to say to him.

Many people, particularly men, feel helpless when someone near to them is emotionally upset. In fact, a man may most often feel threatened or afraid. When someone he loves is sad, angry, hurt, or really afraid, he wants to "make it all better" somehow or make his spouse's feelings go away. He tries to *do* something about his spouse's condition by saying something like, "Don't worry about it. It's going to be all right. There is nothing to be concerned about. Don't cry. It's going to be okay." Although his intention may be to soothe and comfort his wife, the message she hears is, "Stop feeling what you feel." The ironic thing is that the more he tries to show his concern in this fashion, the more frustrated he becomes since his efforts do not seem to change anything.

The good husband doesn't resort to reason in the face of emotion because he is stupid or because he is deliberately trying to make his wife feel bad. On the contrary, it is a learned pattern of behavior, the socially acceptable way for a man to cope with feelings. In truth, he may feel threatened by his wife's feelings because he is uncomfortable with his own. He may not allow himself to express his feelings through crying or by telling another person he is afraid or angry or hurt. When his wife expresses these feelings, she is showing him something that he may not want to see or feel in himself. It is as if he were looking in a mirror and doesn't want to see what is reflected back at him, so he pushed the mirror away. When trying to reason away his wife's emotions, he is also trying to comfort himself. In this exaggerated illustration, the wife is crying, and the husband is trying to comfort her: "Here, dear. Here's a Kleenex. Please stop crying. It's going to be okay. Stop crying. Will you stop crying, please! If you don't stop crying, I won't be able to talk to you!" All his efforts go not into acknowledging her feelings, but into getting her to stop her expression of them. He wants her to stop crying and "be reasonable," because if she doesn't, he might start crying—and he couldn't bear that. He wants to stifle her tears to stop the expression that is bringing him so much discomfort. Such a man is seldom conscious about his motives, but if asked how he feels when his wife cries, he probably would say that he is *uncomfortable*.

Emotions are effectively handled not by shutting them down, but by encouraging their expression. Reason is hardly a good tool for doing this. By verbally acknowledging your partner's feelings, you tell him or her that it is okay to express emotions, and this acknowledgment implies that you are accepting rather than judging your partner's feelings. Husbands, in particular, are afraid to encourage their wives to become more expressive about their emotions. Their fear comes from being taught that they have to *do* something about their wives' emotions, and they don't know what to do. The average man is caught in a bind between wanting to be sensitive to his wife's needs and, at the same time, wanting his wife not to threaten him with more emotion than he can handle.

One of the most difficult things in counseling is convincing men and women that they really don't have to *do* anything with their spouses' emotions. The only thing any of us can do is to *be* there for our partners and to support them. *Being* and *doing* are quite different. One cannot take responsibility for another person's feelings. It not only doesn't work, but it is destructive. When you try to take responsibiity for other people's feelings, they stop doing what is necessary to bring themselves comfort, and because that comfort never really comes, they may blame you for its absence. In the long run, a misplaced sense of responsibility leads to misplaced blame, a deep sense of disappointment, and a lack of self-trust for everyone. However, giving a person assurance that you'll "stay by them" through emotional periods provides that person with the security he or she needs to resolve emotional problems.

To be supportive to one's spouse sounds nice as a concept, but what does it mean in terms of your everyday life? Let us imagine that my wife is upset, that she is hurting emotionally and is crying because her sister was just injured in an auto accident. I want to be there for her. The best way for me to do that is to listen to her and acknowledge her feelings when she talks or just hold her when she cries. In no way should I try to change her feelings. Only she can do that. I also wouldn't want her to stop expressing how she feels until she is ready to stop. I recognize that to "bottle up" any of her emotions could be harmful to her. I do whatever I can to encourage her to express her feelings as much as she wants, knowing that I do not have to *do* anything about them except listen and acknowledge her experience. Not taking responsibility for her emotions doesn't mean I don't care. On the contrary, it means I'm not trying to do the impossible. If she tells me something I can do that would help her, other than listening or holding her, that's a different story. In that case, she is taking responsibility for her feelings by expressing her specific wants or needs.

A Vocabulary of Intimacy

Effective listening sounds easy on paper, but in a real-life situation it becomes more difficult. Many people who try to apply this knowledge find it so difficult that they give up in frustration. So that this won't happen to you, let us explore some important and common barriers that stand in the way of success.

Many people have a limited emotional vocabulary and/or little awareness of their own emotions. Both of these are important in developing the ability to listen effectively. Before people can be sensitive to their mates' emotions, they must be in touch with their own. When I am listening to my wife describe a situation to me, I ask myself, "What emotion would I feel in the situation she is describing?" As soon as I can get in touch with that feeling in me, I can feed that information back to her, and she can see whether or not I'm following her. In order to do this, I need to know my feelings and be able to express them. Everyone has the ability to get in touch with their feelings—it is just a matter of wanting to.

Having the words to name or describe a wide range of feelings is an essential part of being an effective listener. If, for example, the only words you have to say are, "You seem angry" or "You seem to feel good," you're going to sound like a broken record—and you won't be able to follow most emotional discussions accurately.

Developing an emotion vocabulary is one way to increase our awareness of feelings. Most men, for example, use only two or three words to indicate what they feel: "good," "bad," and perhaps, "angry." A good way to increase your emotion vocabulary is to sit down and list as many human emotions as you can think of. These words will not only make you a more effective listener, but will also allow you to broaden your own emotional experiences, making your life infinitely richer.

You Don't Have to Agree in Order to Listen

Another thing that makes effective listening difficult is the belief that when you listen, you must *agree* with everything the speaker says. This belief invariably leads to yelling matches, frazzled nerves, and frustration. I'm not sure of the origins of this belief, but it's a false one. Agreement is not essential to effective listening. I can listen to my wife for an hour, thinking to myself that I disagree with what she is saying. As a listener, I am trying to hear what she is *feeling*—and that's all. My role is to listen to and understand what she is saying. *Agreement* and *understanding* are different. You can understand someone and yet not agree with them at all.

While listening effectively, I may not agree with what my wife is saying, but there is always one aspect of her communication that I had better agree with—and that's her feelings. The rest of what she is expressing may be her opinions, and I might have different ones, but her emotions are *facts*. There is no debate about their validity—they just need to be acknowledged.

How to Listen When Your Mate Is Angry with You

The hardest but most important time to listen effectively is when your spouse is upset with you. Often our first reflex when we hear our mates express disapproval of us is to become defensive. We feel hurt and angry when people we love are upset with us. Besides, we are taught to "stand up" for ourselves when we are attacked. Not to defend yourself is thought to be a sign of weakness in the face of which we suspect others will lose respect for us. In an intimate relationship, these false beliefs can result in poor communication and deep frustration, and lead to psychological as well as physical battles in which everyone ends up a loser.

In any marital relationship, defensiveness and aggressiveness are signs of weakness, not strength. Having to defend and justify yourself indicates an absence of self-confidence with regard to the issue at hand. It takes a great deal of strength not to get sucked in and start defending yourself when you're attacked. A good example of this can be seen in the varying approaches of automobile salespeople. The stereotypical used car salesperson has to use a lot of "hype" to make the cars look good. A new Porsche salesperson just gives out facts and figures, and uses a low-key sales pitch, because the car speaks for itself. The difference between the two salespeople is confidence. When people in intimate relationships feel they have to "sell" or defend and justify themselves, it may be that they lack confidence in their opinions, behavior, or attitudes.

Learning to trust yourself and listen effectively, even when your mate is criticizing or attacking you, is a sign of inner security and emotional self-confidence. If you place a high value on intimacy in your marriage, then the reward for listening is going to be far greater than the reward for defending yourself.

A Time to Listen and a Time to Seek Solutions

Many people make the mistake of trying to offer advice of solutions while their spouses are trying to express feelings about a problem they're having with the marriage. You may have the best intentions, offering these solutions because you care about your mate and want to help. But the question is: did your partner ask for solutions or advice, or did he or she just want you to listen? Most likely your mate just wanted a "sounding board" so he or she could become clearer about the problem. A person who wants to be listened to, but gets advice or solutions instead, will invariably get angry. And, in the process, the advice-giver will probably feel rejected and frustrated. A moment later, the advice-giver may get angry and either walk away or start verbally attacking the person who originally just needed a good listener. In the midst of this, the original topic of discussion gets lost.

Sometimes spouses will feel inadequate because they don't have solutions to the problems their mates present to them. Because they feel inadequate they may refuse to talk about that subject. And if a partner with a problem mistakes his or her spouse's feeling of inadequacy for indifference, that partner may go outside the marriage to find someone else who will listen and care. This is the background for many love triangles, which, of course, can be extremely destructive in a marriage.

A good rule to follow when someone you care for comes to you with a problem is to *listen* and give advice only if asked for it. In this way, you will protect yourself from having your advice rejected when it is not wanted. In addition to protecting yourself from rejection, you will protect your loved one from your own impulse to "rescue" him or her when he or she is in trouble. Remember that comfort comes only through the confidence that grows as one experiences how it feels to solve one's own problems.

In effective listening, a person's total attention is required. Distractions, such as the newspaper, the television, or the kids, must not be allowed. If it becomes necessary to go into another room or take a walk together to isolate yourselves from family distractions, do not hesitate to do so. It tells your mate in a very real way that you care and goes a long way toward building intimacy. Once the distractions have been minimized, one must *want* to listen in order to do so effectively. It is pretty easy to tell when a person isn't paying attention. And as soon as the listener's lack of interest becomes apparent, the person who is trying to be heard will often get angry, feeling that the listener doesn't care.

Effective listening is a demanding activity. As a marriage counselor, it is one of my major tools. Imagine, then, the problems that spouses of people in my profession have. Let me tell you a story about myself, since it illustrates a solution to a problem that all people face when they return home after a hard day at the office.

After listening to my clients all day, you can imagine how receptive I might be to hearing my wife's problems when I get home. As a concerned husband, I want to listen to her and show her that I care, but what I would really like to do is take a shower, get something to eat, read the paper, and be by myself to relax. Instead of doing these things, I used to try to listen to my wife, but I had a difficult time concentrating on what she was saying. She would sense that I wasn't listening and become agitated because it appeared to her that I didn't really want to hear what she was saying. This wasn't true. I did want to hear what she had to say, but not when I first walked in the door after so many hours of counseling. I tried to resolve this problem by taking care of her need to be listened to before I took care of my own needs, but this didn't work because I began to resent having my own needs put off.

The approach that seems to work best is to take care of my own needs—but not before I have *acknowledged* hers. When I come home from work, I say, "I really do want to hear about your day, but first I need to change my clothes and have something to eat. Let's sit down together after dinner so we can really talk." Usually she is willing to wait because she knows she will get my best attention after I've had a chance to unwind. But sometimes she can't wait, and then I make it a point to listen. Since this situation is rare, I can give myself at those times, but I certainly couldn't do it every day. When you learn to acknowledge another person's need with a promise that you'll listen to him or her later, that person feels that you care, that he or she is not being pushed away. However, always follow through with your promise to listen later or this tool for effective listening will become a way of avoiding your mate and you'll lose credibility in your mate's eyes.

"You're Getting Upset over Nothing"

Sometimes your spouse may seem overly emotional about a problem he or she is expressing, and you are unable to imagine how the event described could cause him or her to be so emotional. The

tendency at such times is to say, "You're getting upset over nothing," or to take the position that this problem doesn't warrant your
full attention. The truth is that when the emotion seems out of
proportion to the event, it is more important than ever to apply
effective listening skills.

When a person's emotional intensity does not seem to correspond to the event that brought on his or her emotion, then it is
best to assume that something else might be causing the emotional intensity. The emotional spouse may not even know what's
making him or her so upset except that it seems to have been
triggered by a particular event.

Let us go back to the couple, Linda and John, described earlier.
And let us imagine that Linda explodes at John, really yelling at
him for leaving his clothes all over the bedroom floor. John might
wonder why Linda is so upset, why she is making such a big deal
about his clothes being on the floor. If, instead of yelling back at
her or telling her that she's being too sensitive, he chooses to
listen effectively to her, he may find tht the subject of clothes on
the floor is only the "tip of the iceberg." What is really bothering
Linda is that she feels she is being taken for granted, that she is
unappreciated. John's leaving his clothes on the floor brings up all
these deeper feelings. At first, Linda herself may not recognize
what's really bothering her, but after her initial emotions are acknowledged, her deeper feelings also come to the surface. When
John acknowledged Linda's emotion, he gave them both the opportunity to get to the bottom of the problem and find effective
solutions. Had he ignored her or fought with her for being "too
emotional," the problem would not have gone away. Her deeper
feelings would surface in another situation, and perhaps she
would blow up because she had to cook a meal the next day or
because no one offered to help set the table. So whenever your
spouse seems to be "overly emotional," assume that something
else is bothering him or her. The only way you can find solutions
is by acknowledging and accepting the intensity of your partner's
emotion until he or she is able to tell you of the deeper concerns at
work.

Listening for Nonverbal Messages

Thus far, our discussion of effective listening has focused on *verbal communication*, but people also communicate nonverbally. Nonverbal communication covers everything from "dirty looks" to slamming doors to withdrawing into stubborn silence. At this point, therefore, let us explore some techniques that are helpful in these situations.

Generally, people respond to nonverbal communication in one of two ways. Either they ask questions about what is causing their partners' behavior, or they avoid and/or ignore their partners. Both responses are frustrating for everyone concerned and ineffective in restoring communication so that the couple can enjoy being intimate. In either case, the spouse on the receiving end of the nonverbal communication fails to acknowledge verbally the emotions of the nonverbal spouse. Remember the principle that when our feelings are not acknowledged, we tend to "turn up the volume." People who act out their emotions will increase the intensity of their behavior until they do feel their emotions have been acknowledged. This increase in intensity can run the gamut, from slamming doors and breaking dishes to making an appointment with a divorce attorney—whatever it takes to make oneself heard. It is as if the nonverbal spouse were saying: "I will make you pay attention to me no matter what I have to do."

An example may help. John comes home and finds his wife, Linda, sitting on the couch, looking depressed, sad, angry, or hurt. John cannot decide which it is, but she isn't saying anything.

John: What's the matter, honey? [No response from Linda.] I said, what's the matter with you, Linda? Did something happen today or are you mad at me for something?

Linda: Nothing is the matter.

John: Something's wrong with you, I can tell. Why don't you tell me what happened that's making you so upset?

Linda: I don't know.

John: You don't know! Oh, that's just great. I had a wonderful day at work today, I come home, and you don't want to talk.

Well, I'm going next door to have a drink with Fred. I'll see you later.

In this exchange, John starts off with questions and continues to ask questions throughout the interaction. He communicates to her that he is more concerned with the *cause* of Linda's emotions than with acknowledging their existence. In reality, Linda's behavior is like a flashing neon sign that reads: "I feel sad," "I feel angry," "I feel hurt." But John doesn't seem to see the sign.

When you ask questions, the nonverbal person tends to become even more nonverbal, perhaps because he or she feels interrogated and put on the defensive. The nonverbal person is already having a hard time talking and doesn't need a spouse probing around with questions. When this happens, the nonverbal person may withdraw all the more.

If John decides to walk away—that is, to go have a drink with Fred—he is becoming as nonverbal as his wife. Although Linda may think he's indifferent to her, John's inner thoughts may be running something like this: "I better leave her alone. She seems really upset. If I try to talk to her, we'll probably get into a fight and I've had a hard day already. Maybe she'll get over it if I just leave her alone."

But, chances are, the whole thing won't just *blow over* if John leaves Linda alone. On the contrary, the situation will *blow up*. For when he leaves her alone, Linda feels hurt and uncared for by her husband. And she may feel like increasing the intensity of her nonverbal behavior until her husband does pay attention to her.

The approach that works with a nonverbal spouse involves the same principles of effective listening that you learned for verbal communication. Instead of acknowledging verbally expressed emotions, the listener acknowledges the emotions expressed in the behavior. So now let us return to my example of John and Linda. John comes home and finds Linda sitting on the couch, looking depressed and angry but refusing to talk about it:

John: Linda, you seem upset about something.
Linda: Yeah.
John: Something seems to be making you angry.

> *Linda:*   Well, I'm not angry. I'm just really disappointed that
> you didn't call me today.
> *John:*   I forgot all about it. I'm sorry. I really am!

Here our hapless husband is beginning to get the idea. He makes
statements to acknowledge that he recognizes his wife is upset,
instead of asking her how she feels. She feels that her feelings
matter to him, that he notices them, and so she feels free to open
up. The couple begins talking, leaving a channel for intimacy
wide open. But, of course, it's not always going to be that easy.
Here's another way the exchange might go:

> *John:*   Linda, you seem upset about something. [No response
> from Linda.] Something seems to be really eating at you.
> *Linda:*   No.
> *John:*   Well, I'd like to talk to you about what you're feeling.
> When you're ready, I'll be in the other room.

In this approach, John acknowledges Linda's nonverbal message,
but that's all. He realizes that Linda, at that moment, is not ready
to talk. He expresses his desire to talk and does not pressure her to
talk to him. When he walks into the next room, he has done all he
can as a caring spouse. It would be difficult for Linda to feel ne-
glected and ignored in this situation because John has acknowledged how she felt and has shown an interest in talking with her.

Most of us would have a difficult time just letting Linda be,
with no explanation about what was bothering her. People who
find this difficult might ask themselves, "Am I really concerned
about how my spouse *feels* or do I want to know if I'm the cause of
the upset?" If you're most concerned about what you might have
done to upset her, the chances are that you'll get into a defensive
posture even before she's told you what she's thinking or feeling.
And that posture has a way of making your worst fears come true.
To prevent the potential problems of a defensive posture, focus on
your mate's feelings, keeping in mind that this focus is the key to
intimate communication.

To summarize, effective listening is the key to intimate communication. It is *active* listening, and it includes the verbal acknowledgment of another's feelings. This active form of listening, a skill

that takes practice and conscious effort to master, requires a person's total concentration. When you first start out, it may seem awkward, gamelike, or even clinical, but *any* change in our habits of living seems that way until it becomes a part of our everyday lives. If people respond by saying, "Cut the psychology crap," or "What book did you read that out of?" they're most likely just uncomfortable because you're not playing the game the way you used to do. As your new techniques become more natural and they bring more comfort and intimacy to your life, criticisms such as these will disappear. After all, it's pretty hard to argue with success!

Two last reminders about effective listening. First, feed back the sender's emotions with some regularity. It is all but impossible to let the speaker talk for ten minutes and then feed back all the emotions he or she expressed in one lump. Second, start all the feedback statements with the words, "you," "you feel," or "you seem to feel." Never use *I* messages when you are trying to listen.

Exercise No. 3: Effective Listening

PURPOSE: To develop skills as a listener.

PREPARATION: Arrange approximately one hour when you and your spouse can be together without interruptions or distractions. Review this chapter during the day, prior to sitting down to do this exercise with your mate.

EXERCISE: Sit down with your spouse and mutually decide upon one subject you'd like to discuss, something in your relationship which upsets one of you and which you'd like to change.

Establish a firm agreement with your spouse that one of you will assume the role of "effective listener" while the other speaks.

The speaker should express his or her thoughts and feelings about the subject until he or she feels satisfied that the subject is covered.

The person in the role of the listener should remember that his or her goal is to acknowledge the emotions of the speaker. If you have any doubts about how to do this, go back and review the guidelines for effective listening given throughout this chapter.

When the first speaker feels satisfied that the subject has been exhausted and feels that he or she has been understood, reverse roles and repeat the exercise.

Do this as many times as you wish, but remember to focus on a single subject each time.

10. Conflict Resolution: Contracts for Harmony

As stated earlier, conflicts in marriage are normal and healthy. A conflict begins when two people want different things, indicating, first and foremost, that they are individuals, not carbon copies of each other. One may want to go to sleep when the other wants to have sex. One may be eager to travel at a time when the other wants to stay at home and make some extra money. Many men and women are afraid of conflict with their spouses. They may be afraid because, as children, they witnessed emotionally painful conflicts between their parents. Or they may be afraid because, as children, they rarely experienced conflicts and haven't the vaguest idea of what to do about them.

No one in our culture is really taught how to resolve conflicts constructively. On the contrary, we are taught indirectly and directly, by teachers and parents, that conflict is bad and should be avoided. As a result, many people find themselves in a psychological bind with their mates. They find themselves in marriages, and potentially good marriages at that, where there are clear-cut differences of opinion between partners. Because they have been taught that it is bad to have conflicts and because they have little or no training in resolving conflicts, they may try to deny their differences, thinking that this is the best way to keep the peace in their marriage. Others try to work out their conflicts on their own, through compromise, subverting their own needs to those of their mates, or any number of other methods, all with varying results.

Before the days of the women's movement, conflict may have been less of a problem in marriage—at least on the surface. The fantasy was that the husband was the boss and his word was law in the family. Therefore, the wife went along with what her husband said and supported him even if she disagreed—at least, she was supposed to. Today, this situation has changed considerably. Married women are no longer willing to be in a partnership that is a 70/30 or 60/40 arrangement where the man dominates. What works today is a 50/50 arrangement. I know very few people who like to be dominated in their married life.

Married couples seldom have clear-cut understandings about how they will handle conflicts between them. Seemingly, they just allow the conflicts to take their natural course. Most businesses are run with greater foresight than most marriages. Partnerships and corporations make legal agreements that spell out how they will mediate, arbitrate, and resolve conflicts in an effective manner. Why shouldn't we have similar understandings and agreements in marriage? Marriage is the most highly charged emotional relationship ever established between people, and yet we don't, as a rule, make any effort to establish a format for working out conflicts in constructive ways.

The greater the emotional intensity, the greater is the need for a format or structure for handling conflicts. Emotional energy is like nuclear energy in that when nuclear energy is released gradually and channeled through a structure, such as a nuclear reactor, it can be constructive and beneficial to mankind. But it can also be used for extremely destructive purposes, as we all know.

Although most couples do not have a well-defined agreement about how they will handle marital conflicts, each couple's conflicts will follow a particular pattern. This pattern is like an unwritten script that the couple follows unconsciously. The issue of each conflict may vary, but the conflict pattern remains the same. These patterns may or may not end up resolving conflicts, but more often than not, the process is time-consuming and emotionally painful.

In my work as a marriage counselor, I find that most people develop a competitive attitude toward their mates. This grows out of the belief that the ultimate settlement of any conflict means that one person must win and the other must lose. If both marriage partners are strong, their fights can go on for hours, sometimes days, until one or the other gives up in frustration. But this method of conflict resolution is based on false myths and can only be destructive where intimacy is involved.

It may be true that on a football field or in a boxing ring, there must be one winner and one loser—but does the same principle apply in marriage? Our society teaches us that we must fight to win in every walk of life. But when one person in an intimate relationship "wins" (get what he or she wants at the expense of his or her spouse), the other loses, or at least feels he or she has lost. But the truth is that in all win/lose situations in marriage, the loser feels hurt and resentful, and this means that even the winner loses. Feelings of resentment, anger, and hurt will eventually be expressed in destructive ways, usually directed at the spouse who thinks he or she has won. The competitive, adversary approach to conflict in marriage drives a wedge between the partners, preventing intimacy and too often resulting in the breakup of the marriage.

The most common example of how winning can lead to the destruction of a marriage is best seen with couples who have played out the traditional marriage fantasy for approximately ten years. Typically, the good wife gives in to her husband whenever a conflict becomes heated. She is the "loser" in the conflicts and experiences emotional pain, but may not realize this until quite late in the marriage. Her pain is sometimes masked by the pride she feels in being a good wife who respects her husband. Here is a clear expression of this fantasy, drawn from Marabel Morgan's *The Total Woman*: "Man and woman, although equal in status, are different in function. God ordained man to be the head of the family, its president, and his wife to be the executive vice-president. Allowing your husband to be your family president is just good business."

Marabel may be right that it is important to have power structure for good business—if indeed it is business you are talking about—but in an intimate, personal relationship, power, control, and domination can only lead to pain. After ten years of giving in, placating, selling out, and losing, the good wife has become resentful of her very life. She begins to express her resentment, usually in the way she relates to her husband. Once this process gets started, the woman's emotional walls break down, and the resentment she has been accumulating as a *loser* pours forth—and her husband feels drowned and surprised, unable to imagine the source of so much anger. He had believed his wife was happy with letting him run the house. The husband may lose his wife, because she may be so full of resentment from all those years of domination that she is just emotionally "burned out" on him. Or, he may find he cannot deal with all her resentment and so he himself leaves the relationship. He may have won all the small battles over the years, but he loses his marriage in the end.

It is easy to see the desire to win operating in the way couples communicate in conflicts. They talk as if they were selling a product (their product being what they want), and they put down their competitor's product (what the spouse wants). A sample dialogue might go something like this:

> *Husband:*   You don't want that. It costs too much, and we have no use for it anyway. What I want is much better. It costs less and we can use it more often.
>
> *Wife:*   Listen, what I want doesn't cost all that much! And anyway, you have to spend a little extra for anything that's good. You are just being cheap. If we get what you want, it will fall apart in no time at all.

And soon the couple is off and running, charging headlong into a big yelling match, with both partners competing to see who can outsell the other. They use every selling technique in the book—logic, persuasion, manipulation, threat, out-right personal attack, pressure—to get what they want.

So what is the alternative? In the next few pages, I will describe a basic process through which conflicts can be resolved in intimate relationships.

How to Understand When You Don't Agree

The first goal in resolving a conflict is to *understand* your mate's wants. But recognize, here, that understanding does not mean *agreement*. You can understand what a person wants without having to agree that he or she should get it. Both partners should thoroughly understand what each one wants, and how they feel about these wants, before they agree to anything.

Let us take an example and use it to illustrate a number of different conflict resolutions: Frank wants to go to Colorado for skiing for Christmas vacation, while his wife, Jane, wants to go to the beach in Hawaii. Frank and Jane are equal partners in their marriage, and neither has more power than the other. They respect each other as equals, and know the emotional cost of one person dominating the other.

In trying to understand what his partner wants, Frank will *listen effectively* about Jane's desire to go to Hawaii for their vacation. After Jane feels that Frank understands what she wants—a process that might take ten minutes or three hours—they reverse roles. Now Jane will effectively listen to what Frank wants until he feels that Jane totally understands why he wants to go skiing, what it means to him, and how he feels about going or not going. They both agreed beforehand that they would allow each other equal listening time and equal time to present their own views before making any final decisions. Jane and Frank have reached the first goal or stage in resolving a conflict. Each can say to the other, "You understand what I want." No agreement has been reached between them yet. There has been no discussion of solutions. They are still one hundred and eighty degrees apart, but they do understand each other's needs.

When unions and mangement have conflicts, or when business partners have a conflict they cannot settle, an outside third party may be brought in to help negotiate a solution. Married couples can go see a marriage counselor, of course, but their relationship will be strengthened if they learn how to negotiate their own conflicts. A good counselor will help a couple learn the skills of conflict resolution.

While trying to understand your spouse's position, you do not interrupt him or her with your own opinions, beliefs, or feelings, nor do you say anything about what you want. You put everything that has to do with your position on hold until your spouse finishes and feels understood. When you reach this position, you can then talk about what you want, and your spouse listens in the same manner that you listened to him or her.

Let us return to Frank and Jane and their conflict about where to go for Christmas vacation. We left them at the first stage of conflict resolution—that is, with mutual understanding. While each understands what the other wants, there is still no final agreement about where they will go.

When a partner fully understands what his or her spouse wants, and how he or she feels about those wants, it becomes much easier to give to that person with no strings attached and no feelings of resentment. Frank might say, "I didn't know that going to Hawaii meant so much to you. I can go skiing locally, but we can't go to the beach around here." The mutual understanding between them has removed the adversary relationship that a power struggle might set up, and alternatives, when both parties feel satisfied, become easier to see.

Solutions, Not Compromises

What if, even after they understand each other, Frank still wants to go skiing in Colorado and Jane still wants to go to the beach in Hawaii? In this case, the next step in conflict resolution is to focus on *mutually* thinking about solutions that *both* people will find satisfying. The problem, as well as the responsibility for resolving it, belongs equally to them both.

The word *compromise* is often used in connection with the process of conflict resolution, particularly in the solution-seeking stage. The common notion about compromise is that each person in the conflict gives up fifty percent of what he or she wants. In this case, each person ends up feeling only partially satisfied— which *can* mean half-satisfied and half-resentful. Which part you focus on is your own choice. As in the ancient parable of the man with half a glass of wine, you can choose to see your glass as half-empty or you can see it as half-full.

Ideal solutions give both people one hundred percent of what they want, and in a few situations, this is possible. Let us suppose that Frank and Jane have a small conflict about where they'll go for dinner one night. Jane wants to go out for pizza and Frank wants to have a steak. To resolve this conflict, they sit down and think of as many possibilities as they can, without rejecting any of them. Some possible solutions might be:

- They could go to a resturant that serves only steak or a restaurant that serves only pizza.
- They could go to separate restaurants, so they could get what
  each wants to eat.
- They could flip a coin, if they're both in a gambling mood.
- They could take turns. This week they could go where Frank
  wants to go, and next week they could go where Jane wants
  to go.
- They could go to a restaurant that serves both steak and
  pizza.

After they have made their list, they go through each possible
solution until they find one they both feel good about. From the
list above, Frank and Jane would probably choose the last one—
that is, they would go to a restaurant that serves what they both
want. With this solution, both partners get one hundred percent
of what they want, and both come away from the conflict feeling
that they have won. This example is rather simplistic, but these
minor conflicts do occur all the time in a relationship. And when a
couple learns to handle the little conflicts, the larger ones will go a
lot easier. Not only will they have gained practice in conflict resolution, but they also will have settled their conflicts equitably
along the way. As a result, there will be no pent-up resentments
from the past that might complicate resolutions to larger conflicts
in the future.

No Unfinished Business

The best rule to follow when resolving a conflict is that no one
leaves the "negotiation table" with feelings of resentment or a
sense that things are not quite settled. Neither spouse wants to
feel "ripped off," taken advantage of, or dominated. If any of these
feelings exist, then the couple needs to go back and find a better
solution. Sometimes the search for a comfortable solution may
take ten minutes; at other times, it may take two weeks. But it is
better to have a solution that really works—even if it takes a lot of
time to work it out—than it is to settle for the first solution presented just to get the matter over quickly.

There is nothing wrong with holding off on a settlement if you or your mate cannot immediately find a workable solution. Some-times it's better to take a break. When you come back to the negoti-ations, you may have a fresher and more objective view of the situation, which might yield new insights into possible solutions. However, if you put the process on hold, do make sure that you get back to resolving the conflict. If saying, "Let's talk about this to-morrow" really means, "Let's drop this forever—it's just too upset-ting," then you are setting yourself up for later problems.

Unresolved conflicts seem to keep coming up in most mar-riages, no matter how long ago they occurred. When these unre-solved conflicts surface, they drive a wedge between the partners, making all levels of intimacy difficult. The more unresolved con-flicts there are in a marriage, the more complicated and painful each new conflict seems to be. Often, a seemingly innocent dis-agreement that goes unresolved can trigger another bigger dis-agreement, which, in turn, sets off another, until the feelings of anger, confusion, and resentment become overwhelming despite efforts to keep them under control. Burying all this "unfinished business" for years causes the basic fabric of the marriage to disin-tegrate. The couple's sex life, the way they spend time together, they way they talk to one another—all aspects of their relation-ship are affected.

Sometimes one partner wants something of the other—using the credit card less, keeping the house cleaner, spanking the kids less—that doesn't lend itself well to the negotiation process. In such a case, the only solution may be to do what the other person asks. But that is seldom as easy as it sounds. We all find ourselves at some time or other resisting change, especially if the change in-volves a habit or a way of being that has been with us a long time. We may resist change from sheer inertia or because we get some sort of satisfaction out of continuing a habit, but in any case, we do well to keep in mind that continuing a habit that irritates one's mate may cause that person's irritation to grow to amazing pro-portions.

When I am counseling a couple with a problem like this, I ask the person who is behaving in the irritating manner, "What do you get out of doing something that causes resentment in your partner?" Most frequently, the answer is, "Nothing." But if that were really the case, then the behavior would already be changed. Usually a person who is reluctant to change sees the change as a step toward losing his or her autonomy. The inner feeling is that the person is afraid of losing control over his or her own life. Such an individual may feel that, "If I give an inch, they'll take a mile." *Understanding* this fear, no matter how illogical or irrational it may seem, allows the person requesting the change to be patient and to recognize that something more than stubbornness is causing his or her mate to resist the change.

At different times in our lives, we are all resistant to change, even the most insignificant ones. Understanding this about yourself, as well as your mate, is part of listening effectively. When you find yourself resisting a change, ask yourself if the change *really* represents a threat to your sense of self or to your autonomy. And keep in mind that the benefits of increased intimacy may be well worth the cost of picking up your clothes or not scattering the newspaper all over the house—whatever the habit is that your mate has asked you to change. And give your mate a little space when he or she seems resistant to these small changes. Avoid becoming defensive or psychologizing if your partner doesn't immediately do what you request. Above all, don't feel that the stubbornness is directed against you. With gentle reminders, most people will work out their resistance on their own, and the changes will come.

Once you've made an agreement with your mate to change a part of your behavior that he or she finds irritating, follow through. Make the change. If you don't, you will create a credibility gap. Agreeing to do something just to appease for the moment, without really intending to change, will backfire later. When an agreement to change is ignored, the problem is compounded. You and your partner are not only in conflict over the original problem, but now a new problem has been created. When credibility and trust are lost, the couple's ability to communicate intimately erodes. Little or no effort is made to work out problems any more because neither partner has much faith in the other to make changes. And so frustration and resentment build, driving an ever-increasing wedge of discontent between husband and wife, robbing them both of the comfort and luxury of intimacy.

Going back to Frank and Jane, let us see what they have done with their conflict about where to go on their vacation. Frank still wants to go skiing in Colorado, and Jane still wants to go to Hawaii. It is now obvious that they cannot both get what they want if each insists on his or her original plans and they take their vacation together. They finally decide to start looking for a third alternative—a place to go that both will be happy with.

As trite as it may sound, marriage *is* a give-and-take situation. Giving without strings or resentment is a gift, one that deserves to be appreciated. Hopefully, giving up something that you value highly in order to resolve a conflict will happen rarely in your life. It is much better to find solutions in which both partners get what they want. If one spouse feels that he or she is doing all or most of the giving, guilt develops on the part of the "taker" and resentment develops on the part of the "giver." And the end result, once more, is that both partners suffer the loss of intimacy.

Often I use an example from my own childhood to illustrate the need for a structure to resolve conflicts. When I was about twelve and my brother was eight, we fought constantly, as most siblings do at those ages. We would fight over who scratched whose records, or who stole the baseball, or who got to use the bike that day—important issues to children. Since I was older and larger, I often used force, or physical intimidation, to get my way at my brother's expense. However, what he lacked in physical strength he made up in mental agility. He got back at me by destroying plastic models I'd made. Eventually I came to realize that no amount of my hitting him was going to make up for the hours I spent building the models he destroyed. At this point, I recognized that my use of power no longer worked, and I began going to my mother, asking for her help as a negotiator. She structured the conflicts, giving my brother and me equal time to speak our minds in the process of working out or conflicts. This was what she called "having court." Without this structure, I ended up having my models destroyed and my brother had to live in fear of my physical threats—a loss for both of us, any way you cut it. The structure my mother taught us eventually brought my brother and me closer together.

To summarize, conflicts in marriage are much more easily resolved when a couple develops a plan or structure for dealing with disagreements. It is important that this plan be one that the partners work out *together*, at a time when they both feel calm, secure, and relatively free of conflicts. Couples should work out their own style in this conflict resolution plan so that it feels *natural* for them. However, as you work out your own plan, be sure to include these three essential stages:

1. *Listen Effectively*: Set up a structure that gives each partner equal time to tell about his or her wants without interruption, judgment of those wants, or implied agreement or disagreement on the part of the listener.

2. *Work Out Solutions Together*: Sit down together and list alternatives or possible solutions, and then concentrate on those that offer *both* you and your partner a good deal.

3. *Don't Rush the Process*: Make certain that both you and your partner leave the "negotiation table" with feelings of completion, with a sense that the conflict is resolved and that no resentments are going to be carried over.

This may seem like a simple plan—and on the surface, it is. But keep in mind that even simple goals can be difficult to reach. It takes time and patience to change old habits. Yet, as you reap the rewards of successfully resolving your marital conflicts, you will find yourself more and more motivated to use the structure you've built for resolving conflicts, and less and less willing to risk damaging the increased intimacy you now enjoy with your mate.

11. Deadly Patterns: Common Roles That Kill Intimacy

Because marriage counselors work with hundreds of couples, they are in a position to see that there are common recurring patterns in the way husbands and wives relate to each other. Just knowing that there are common patterns, and being able to recognize when you and your spouse are caught up in one, gives you the choice of continuing your marriage that way or seeking alternatives to improve things. It is hard to change when you don't know what the problem is. And even if you don't find yourself in any of the patterns discussed in this chapter, you will still benefit from learning about them. The new knowledge will hopefully keep you from falling into these traps.

Generally, it takes only one spouse to break a relationship pattern. When one changes, the other is forced to do something different because his or her partner is no longer playing the game. So let us look now at some of the common behavioral patterns that cause problems in marriage.

The Parent-Child Pattern

This pattern is the most common one in marriage. What occurs is that one spouse consistently communicates to the other in a parental way. Usually, the communication is critical or judgmental and takes the form of *you* messages.

The pattern usually starts with one spouse telling that he or she should do something. In this case, let us suppose that Jane, one partner in the couple from the preceding chapter, says to her husband, Frank, "You should spend more time with our children," or "You shouldn't let your boss push you around so much," or "You always leave your clothes all over the place."

What Jane is saying, on one level, is that Frank needs to be helped along, that he needs the kind of guidance a child needs. Most adults do not like to be told what to do, unless they specifically request that information. And certainly no self-respecting adult likes to be talked to as if he or she were a child. So when Frank's wife talks this way to him, most likely he will feel angry and hurt.

Jane is probably not trying to make her husband feel uncomfortable. More likely, she is worried about something he's doing and would like him to change. But even though Jane's motives may be good—that is, she feels she's telling him something that could improve his life—Frank can easily take her message as meaning that she thinks he is inadequate. It is this indirect message that Frank reacts to emotionally, and so he most likely will be unable to acknowledge her underlying care and concern because he resents the implications of her suggestion so much.

At this point, Frank will most likely do one of two things: either he will act out his feelings, or he will respond as a critical parent. Both of these choices deserve to be considered in some detail.

First, how might Frank *act out* his feelings? He might withdraw, get sullen, slam a door, do the opposite of what Jane suggested, be moody, and so on. Maybe when Frank was a child, there was a rule in his family that children should not express the so-called negative emotions because his parents considered this "sassy" or "talking back." Whenever Frank violated this rule, he was probably punished. So, in order to avoid punishment, he learned to suppress his anger and began to act out his feelings through slamming doors, sulking, or whatever other methods he could get away with, instead of verbalizing what he felt.

What happens when Frank follows the same response pattern as an adult? Primarily, he loses self-esteem because now he is an adult acting like a teenager. In addition, when Frank responds in a childlike manner, he indirectly tells Jane that he is indeed still a child who needs to be told how to run his life. The more he expresses his anger in this way, the more he encourages Jane to act like a parent. And Jane, unaware of how much her reaction encourages his childlike actions, feels she must tell him what to do, feels her guidance is necessary. This idea sets her up for becoming not only a rescuer, but eventually a persecutor, chastizing him when she finally becomes sick and tired of being a mother to her husband.

The second way that Frank might express his anger is by responding to Jane like a critical parent, giving her "a bit of her own medicine." That exchange might go something like this:

Jane: Frank, you should be more careful when you drive on the freeway.

Frank: Oh yeah? Well, you don't drive all that great either. The way you drive, you're lucky the highway patrol hasn't locked you up.

Jane: Well, at least I don't have any speeding tickets! You should slow down!

Frank: I should slow down!? You're the one with the lead foot, not me.

If this dialogue continued, it is likely that Frank and Jane would end up in a big argument and finally, out of frustration, stop talking to each other. Once again, Jane and Frank reinforce each other's parent and child patterns of relating. When Jane talks to Frank like a critical parent, he gets angry and talks to her the same way. In turn, she gets angry at being treated like a child and gets even more critical and parental. The longer this goes on, the higher the volume and intensity, until what began as a suggestion has turned into a free-for-all.

It is important to remember that it only requires one person to break the pattern. However, if both people together decide to stop engaging in their parent-child roles, the change will happen quicker and be longer-lasting.

The longer a behavioral pattern like this has been operating, the more automatic it becomes and the harder it is to change, but a person can change whenever he or she chooses to do so. All one needs is: (1) awareness of the behavior pattern operating, (2) the desire to change, and (3) a more effective style of communication to replace the old pattern.

Leaving Home: Alternatives to the Parent-Child Roles

Couples who change the parent-child patterns in their marriages often report that they find themselves relating differently to their parents as well. This is not at all unusual, as my own case might illustrate.

When I was a child, I was able to express my emotions and opinions openly. Usually I did so in a childlike manner, attacking and defending. Even though I was able to express myself, I still respected my parents' authority, although the neighbors may not have thought so, judging by all the noise that came from our house.

However, all this ended for me when I went away to college. There I started taking responsibility as an adult. I didn't have anyone telling me what I should do all of the time. When I came home during vacation breaks, the parent-child pattern still maintained by my parents—who didn't yet see that I'd grown up—became uncomfortable. The moment I walked into the house, I became tense and defensive. I got the feeling that my mother was never going to acknowledge the fact that I'd grown up. In her mind, I was still her child, and she was still going to relate to me as a parent by telling me what I should do: "Dan, you should get your hair cut," or "Your car doesn't sound very good. Maybe you should get it looked at," or "You should be eating better." My response to these well-meaning statements was to react as I had when I was a teenager: "Mom, you don't know what you're talking about," or "You don't know what it's like at college, since you have never been there." And soon we were fighting just as we had when I was younger. I was quite frustrated by this situation, since I had come to think of myself as an adult. Here I was, twenty-three years old and acting just like a sixteen-year-old kid.

When vacation ended, I returned to school, where I became acutely aware of how I had fallen back into my patterns of behavior while I was home. I wanted to change this. I didn't like being an *adolescent* twenty-three-year-old man. I couldn't accept that image of myself. I promised myself that when I went home again, I would not get pulled into a child relationship with my parents. I knew it wouldn't be easy. It would take a great deal of conscious effort to make this change.

Whenever my mother started telling me what to do, I planned to respond to her as an adult. Instead of expressing my anger at being treated like a child—yelling and counterattacking as I had when I was a child—I decided I would communicate my emotions in a responsible, clear, adult manner. I would use *I* messages.

My first attempts with *I* messages went something like this: "Mom, I really resent it when you keep telling me how I should look or what I should wear. I don't mind you expressing your opinions, but don't tell me what I should do all the time." In the beginning, I made one major error: I didn't acknowledge the caring aspect of her parental statements. As a result, my mother felt hurt and rejected. To make it clear that I was not rejecting her, but only wanted to express my ideas in an adult manner, I told her, "Mom, I really appreciate your worrying about the way I'm eating or whether my car is operating correctly, but I really resent it when you tell me how I should run my life." At this point, she began to see me in a different light. She couldn't feel that I didn't appreciate her concern for me, because I had acknowledged that I did. She soon began relating to me as an adult. The old system had been broken and a new pattern was established.

Some parents want to relate to their grown children as adults. Others fight to the end to maintain their old parent-child relationships with their offspring. If your parents fall into the latter category, it is important to know that *you* don't have to remain a child, even if they treat you that way. In my own case, my mother wanted to change. It took her a while, but since I was consistent in my new style of communication, it wasn't long before we were able to establish a healthy adult relationship.

This same type of change can occur in a marriage. Usually, a married couple has less difficulty making the change because the length of time that the pattern has been in operation is not as long as it is in a parent-child relationship. Whereas a growing child needs parental guidance, adult men and women don't. Indeed, husband and wife will find their lives much easier if they relate as the equal adults they are.

But, you may ask, how can you give your wife or husband a suggestion without seeming like a critical parent? There is nothing wrong with making suggestions—as long as they are wanted. Parents don't ask their children if they would like their advice. Frequently this habit spills over into adult relationships. To avoid sounding like a parent, ask your mate if he or she would like a suggestion. Giving your mate a choice shows that you respect him or her as a responsible adult. Not incidentally, it also prevents resentment from developing when that person doesn't want your advice.

Thus, it is important to remember two things in connection with the parent-child pattern: first, *you* messages tend to start and perpetuate it, and, second, *I* messages break the pattern.

Passive and Aggressive Pitfalls

These two words, *passive* and *aggressive*, help us understand a wide range of behavior patterns. They describe attitudes or styles of relating to others. Becoming aware of the drawbacks, as well as the benefits of each style, can help a person choose an effective way of being in the world.

Let us look first at the passive style of relating. This is the classic "nice guy" posture. Passive people are seemingly "easy-going" and adaptive. Though others may find them easy to get along with, the truth is that they deny their own wants or needs. They let other people go first, or do what other people want, even though they may want something different. Passive people feel inhibited around other people and do not communicate intimately. They may talk a lot, but they rarely disclose their true feelings and desires. Emotionally, they feel hurt and anxious much of the time, but they try not to reveal these feelings. They feel hurt because they do not take care of themselves by asking to get their needs or wants met—instead, they allow others to step on them. They feel anxious, worrying that their true feelings might be expressed and their facade broken. They literally "put on an act," especially for those people closest to them. Because they feel they must act, they tend to be in a constant state of performance anxiety, similar to the way actors feel before they go out on stage. They find it difficult to relax, always anticipating their next command performance. Passive people avoid making choices or expressing what they like. They are apt to say, "Whatever you would like to do, honey," or "Whatever you want to do will be fine." Passive people rarely get what they want or need. Since they never tell people what they want, their needs can only be fulfilled by chance.

The partners of passive people may feel both guilty and angry about their mates' behavior style. At first, they feel guilty because they're getting everything they want and they see their spouses aren't getting anything. Because the passive person *seems* easy-going and adaptable, a relationship with him or her is seductive— at least in the beginning. But the more aggressive spouse often begins to feel guilty because the passive mate is so "nice," so "generous," while the more aggressive or demanding partner doesn't feel he or she is reciprocating.

After a while, however, the more aggressive partner becomes angry and resentful, feeling that he or she must always take responsibility for decisions. At the point when the more aggressive partner becomes fed up with his or her mate's consistently passive attitude, a dialogue might go like this:

"Where do you want to go for dinner?"

"Wherever you want to go will be fine."

"No, I'm asking you: what do you want to eat tonight?"

"I had no particular food in mind. Whatever suits your taste."

"No, look, I'm getting tired of always having to make the choices around here. Will you just pick a restaurant for a change?"

"Okay. How about Chinese?"

"Thank you."

A person living with a passive spouse may not only feel angry and guilty, but after a while will lose respect for that spouse and begin to run him or her down. It's difficult to respect people who let others walk all over them. If, for example, a husband is always giving in to his wife's needs at the expense of his own, she will eventually take him for granted or always come to expect that she will get her own way. Similarly, I have had many husbands tell me that they enjoy the security they have with their passive wives, but that they are also very bored with them. This sort of husband finds himself attracted to more assertive women—often a person he meets at work. Although he may entertain an affair with her, he would not want to live with her because she intimidates him. A husband may feel so little respect for his passive wife that he is blind to what she gives him in the relationship. He believes she will always be there, giving generously of herself, not matter how little he gives in return. And, of course, the passive wife does little to challenge this belief. Husbands can also be passive, but far more often it is the wife who plays this role.

The aggressive type, the second of the two styles of behavior, is the complete opposite of the passive type. In marriage, aggressive people are self-enhancing at the expense of their spouses. They appear to have a single interest in life—getting what they want or need. If they have to step on others to get it—well, that's just the way it goes. Although such people may apologize for their behavior, they do so only after they get what they want. Aggressive people appear to have no inhibitions. When they communicate verbally with their spouses, it is most often in a condescending, critical, dictatorial, or "put-down" style. Such people allow no room for a decision-making process when conflicts arise with their spouses. They are the "head of the house," the boss, the dictator, the final authority. They choose for others. Instead of saying, "Whatever you would like, honey," they say "This is what *we* are going to do tonight." Aggressive people in marriage get what they want and need, but usually not without hurting their partners.

The spouses of aggressive people are going to feel deprived, because it seems that their wants are of no importance whatsoever to their mates. What they want is usually nothing more than an obstacle to be removed. The aggressive person's style of communication causes his or her spouse to feel judged, defensive, and humiliated. Being involved with an aggressive person means that you seldom, if ever, get what you want or need. You end up feeling hurt and angry.

To many people, being passive or aggressive are the only two choices available in marriage. And, not surprisingly, people seem to get stuck in these two roles even when they are aware of them.

Part of the reason this happens is that these styles of relating correspond to the sex-role stereotypes of our culture: the aggressive man and the passive woman.

A passive man is "not masculine" and might be regarded as henpecked or a spineless milquetoast. An aggressive woman is likely to be characterized as unfeminine, a dyke, a ball-breaker, or a castrating bitch.

Many times I see people switch back and forth from passive to aggressive. They develop a great deal of resentment after being "nice" or passive for a while. Then, when their resentment level has reached the "full" mark, they switch and become aggressive, letting out all their resentment and anger. But then, after acting in the aggressive manner for a while, they may feel guilty about being so abrasive and dominating. So, they go back to being "nice," repeating the pattern all over again.

Self-Assertion: A Key to Marital Harmony

The alternative to passive and aggressive roles is assertiveness. *Assertiveness* is a popular term, but I find that many people who use the word are confused about what it really means. Many times, they confuse aggressive behavior with assertive behavior. As a consequence, it is common to associate being assertive with being selfish, dominating, or pushy—all adjectives that appropriately describe aggressive people, but have little to do with assertiveness.

To help clear up this confusion, I want to describe some of the main aspects of assertive behavior. People who act assertively do so to enhance themselves, but they do not seek this enhancement at the expense of their partners. They don't bulldoze their wants, ignoring the needs of others as they charge blindly forward. Aggressive people seem to ignore their partners' feelings, while assertive people value the feelings of their mates and give them room in all decisions. Assertive people communicate verbally, making their wants and needs known without forcing anyone to accept them.

Assertive people choose only for themselves. Instead of saying, "Oh, whatever you would like, honey," or "We are going to do this tonight," an assertive person would say,"I would like to go to a movie with you. Is there one you'd particularly like to see?" Plenty of space is given for the partner to express his or her own desires.

Assertive people express what they want clearly and directly, but they do not assume they will always get what they want. Instead, they express their wants in the spirit of negotiation, *hoping* they will get what they want, but knowing that there are never any guarantees.

Because assertive people are accustomed to giving space to others' wants and needs, being the mate of an assertive person means that you can be assertive, too. In theory, assertive behavior begets assertive behavior. In practice, this may not be quite as true, because passive people frequently feel threatened by people who make their needs known and expect others to do the same. We must accept the fact that some passive people dread the opportunity to express themselves. Similarly, assertive and aggressive people don't get along well because aggressive people have a need to dominate others, something that they just can't do with a person who is assertive.

What You Get for Being Passive, Aggressive, or Assertive

When looking at what it is like to be passive, you might ask yourself why a person would want to be that way. Or, as I ask my students and clients, "What is the psychological payoff for being passive?" On the surface, there would seem to be no payoff—but that's not the case.

If you are married to a passive person, you cannot have a conflict with him or her. Every time there is a difference of opinion, your passive partner gives in, going along with whatever you want. The passive person's goal is to avoid conflict, to "get along."

Why are confrontation and conflict so threatening to passive partners that they deny themselves just to keep peace in a marriage? Two basic fears lead people to become passive. The first is the fear of loss and rejection. Passive people often fear that unless they agree with their spouses, their partners will leave them and find others who will treat them better or who will be "nicer." The second fear is that if they let their spouses know their real feelings, desires, and opinions, their mates won't love them and will want to find others. These fears may not be *logical*, and frequently they have no grounds in reality, but they nonetheless have a powerful effect on the passive person's relationships with others. It is as though the passive person has a little voice inside that says, "They wouldn't like you if they knew what you were really like."

A passive person's fears make it almost impossible to be intimate with them. They rarely let you know what's really going on with them. You're never sure when they're telling you what they want and when they're just telling you what they believe you want to hear. In other words, you can never know these people because they are afraid to tell you who they really are.

At this point, let us go back for a moment to our stereotype of the good wife in traditional marriage fantasies. The good wife tries to keep her husband happy and doesn't want to create conflicts in her marriage. Being passive is a perfect solution for her. She denies herself and doesn't let her husband know who is really behind this good-wife facade. No wonder that, after a while, all the husband can feel is that he "appreciates" his wife for all the things she does for him—cooking, cleaning, raising the kids, and entertaining. Not that there is anything wrong with his appreciating these qualities, but they may have little if anything to do with this woman's own wants or needs. The qualities that make her the *person* she is exist outside her good-wife role and would include such things as her sense of humor, her intellectual abilities, and her sexuality. How can her husband appreciate these qualities if she never expresses herself around him? And how can she enjoy her own existence if she always keeps herself hidden?

The consequences of the good-wife charade are twofold. First, her husband doesn't really know her, even after ten years of marriage. And second, as a result of being passive for ten years, the good wife is filled with resentment at having denied herself for so long.

When the good wife's passive facade finally breaks down, as it so often does in counseling, her husband often feels threatened, overwhelmed, and confused. I can't tell you how many times I've heard husbands tell their wives, "Why didn't you tell me about the things that bothered you?" or "I don't really know the person I've been married to all these years. I thought you were happy all this time." As the good wife starts aggressively expressing her resentments, her husband may react defensively and get angry with her for changing. This, of course, intensifies the conflict. Couples who are unwilling or unable to make the adjustments may separate at this point. Ironically, the fear that motivated the wife's passive role—that is, the fear of losing her husband—has caused what she was afraid of to come true.

Passive people generally have low self-esteem, especially about their capacities as spouses. A vicious circle is established. Because they have low self-esteem, passive people let others walk on them, which in turn causes them to feel even lower. In a misguided effort to be accepted by others, they become even more passive— which wins them only further abuse. The longer a person remains passive, the lower his or her self-esteem drops—and the lower his or her self-esteem drops, the more passive that person becomes.

The lower an individual's self-esteem is upon entering a marriage, the greater the chance is that he or she will fall into the passive cycle. This is particularly true for women, while men with low self-esteem upon entering marriage tend to become aggressive.

But enough about passive behavior. Aggressive behavior also inhibits the development of intimacy in marriage. After all, who in their right mind would open up emotionally to a person who is going to judge, criticize, and humiliate? No one—unless they were actually seeking out psychological pain. Instead of allowing themselves to be vulnerable by telling their mate how they feel, people married to aggressive spouses will build psychological walls around themselves for protection, thus making intimacy unlikely.

Just as passive people hold back, aggressive people rarely communicate information that will make them vulnerable. They may talk a lot, but if they talk about their marriages it will usually be to communicate their opinions about their spouses or about what they themselves want.

The *you* message is the aggressive person's favorite method of communicating because everyone else, particularly his or her spouse, is the favorite topic for "discussion." Through the use of *you* messages, aggressive people can be critical, dictatorial, and judgmental, without disclosing anything about themselves. When aggressive people want to express what they want, they will stop using *you* only long enough to say "I want."

Aggressive people's low self-esteem is usually well hidden behind a facade of opinions, cockiness, and what often passes for self-assurance. Most of what they express is designed to keep others from knowing how inadequate they really feel. The behavior of aggressive people is generally just offensive enough to keep others from wanting to know what they are really like, and that is exactly what they want. The cost, of course, is that aggressive people end up feeling lonely.

Aggressive people are often aware of the flaws in their style of relating to others. Of course, they would never admit to their feelings of inadequacy because that might put a crack in the facade. This self-judgment evokes guilt, which, in turn, causes many aggressive people to switch to being passive, at least for a while.

Intimacy Based on Assertion

Assertive behavior, unlike the other two behavior patterns, fosters intimacy in a marital relationship. Assertive people express what is true for them in terms of their feelings and desires. By expressing this information without pushing, forcing, or judging their mates, assertive people make themselves psychologically vulnerable, thus making it possible for their spouses to become intimate with them. The atmosphere in the relationship becomes safe for their spouses. Being assertive doesn't guarantee that the other person in the relationship will become intimate, but it does give the couple a chance—unlike the other two behavioral patterns.

The high self-esteem of the assertive person fosters even higher self-esteem. What happens with assertive behavior is, not surprisingly, the reverse of what happens with nonassertive—that is,

passive or aggressive—behavior. The more people express themselves in an assertive way, the better they are going to feel about
themselves. The higher your self-esteem, the easier it is for you to
be clear and decisive in your relations with other people, particularly your spouse. So assertive behavior and self-esteem build on
each other in a positive, upward spiral.

It is not always easy to become an assertive person, and the
lower one's self-esteem, the more difficult the change. It is a real
psychological challenge. If, for example, you have always been
passive, and you decide to become assertive, your spouse is going
to have to make some radical changes. These won't be comfortable
at first. We all resist change to one degree or another, and this
resistance often takes some unpleasant forms. For example, your
mate may find it difficult to be supportive of your efforts to
change. You may have to confront sarcasm, criticism, and emotional withdrawal—all of which hurt emotionally. But the hurt
felt from a threatened spouse is far less destructive than the self-
imposed pain of low self-esteem suffered by passive people.

The Bitch and the Nice Guy

After seeing hundreds of couples, I have noticed a certain pattern
that, for purposes of vivid illustration, is best described in stereotypes: the bitch and the nice guy. An example of a dialogue that
involve this pattern might start when the husband, Frank, comes
home from work and discovers that his wife, Jane, is very upset
about something he did before he left for work:

Frank: Hi, Jane. How was your day?
Jane: Do you know what you did this morning?
Frank: No, but I can tell you're upset about it.
Jane: I'm so angry with you!
Frank: Now, dear, let's talk about this calmly. Let's sit down in
the living room and discuss it.
Jane: Talk about it calmly? I've got a perfect right to be upset
with you! [Her voice gets louder.]
Frank: Now, nothing can be accomplished by being so irratio-
nal. If you want to talk to me, you've got to stop yelling. [He
starts to walk away.]

> *Jane:* You're not listening to me! What do you think I am, a computer? I'm angry, Frank, and I . . ."
>
> *Frank:* [Interrupting Jane.] I'm going next door until you calm down. [He leaves.]
>
> *Jane:* Oh, sure, just walk out when I'm angry at you! Come back here! [Yelling out the door.]

Now, the neighbors across the street hear this argument between Frank and Jane, and they say to each other, "Poor Frank. He's such a nice guy, so easy-going, and he has to live with that woman. She's such a bitch." The problem is that both Frank and Jane agree with the neighbors' perceptions. Frank sees himself as being okay, the nice guy in this situation. He pats himself on the back for not losing his temper, for being able to keep his cool. Meanwhile, Jane puts herself down for the way she has acted and is disgusted at what she has become in her marriage, the stereotypical "nagging bitch." Her self-esteem is in the gutter. She believes something is wrong with her, and maybe she ought to see a marriage counselor. Frank is such a nice guy. He deserves better treatment.

Frank and Jane don't see that they *both* contribute to this behavioral pattern. If either one were to change, the psychologically painful pattern would be broken.

What is really going on? First, Frank has a difficult time dealing with his wife's feelings of anger and resentment. More often than not, Frank has difficulty acknowledging Jane's anger because he can't acknowledge or accept his own. It's as if Jane were holding up a mirror and showing Frank something about himself that he doesn't want to acknowledge. Therefore, he wants to withdraw from his wife when she becomes emotional. He fears that if he himself becomes angry or emotional, he will lose control and hurt his wife. He is afraid of his anger, and he tells himself that he should control himself at all times. The message he sends Jane is the same one he imposes on himself: block your emotions and be rational.

Because he is afraid of confronting Jane's feelings and his own, he physically withdraws. This upsets Jane even more—which, in turn, increases Frank's anxiety. He has not only fanned the flames of a relatively small emotional fire, he has poured fuel on it.

Though his role in the flare-up is subtle, he is no less responsible for it than his wife.

Jane could learn to communicate her feelings in a way that wouldn't cause Frank to want to control them. She might try using *I* messages, instead of dumping her emotions on Frank and attacking him through *you* messages. Although one cannot expect a spouse to use *I* messages all the time, it is beneficial to both if, when one spouse is emotionally upset, the other can remain emotionally centered. Jane could also see how she gets "sucked in" by Frank's stubborn insistence on rational discussion and/or his withdrawal from her at the moment she most needs him to listen. If she could realize that it is his inability to deal with anger, not his indifference to her, that causes him to seek reason and/or withdraw, she might not feel rejected by his behavior, and her pattern of playing the "bitch" role would diminish.

The Pinprick Pattern

The pinprick pattern goes like this: Let us pretend that I have a sharp sewing pin in my hand, and I start sticking you in the leg with it ever so lightly, without knowing I'm doing it. This might hurt you a little bit, but you don't want to tell me about it, because it's such a small irritation and in all other ways we are getting along well. To comment on it would seem petty. Not knowing that I'm hurting you, I continue to stick you with this pin. Your response, after a period of time, will probably follow one of two paths. First, you might explode in anger and yell, "Will you quit sticking me with that damn pin!" I might respond by sticking you harder, becaue now I'm mad at you for yelling at me. Or, second, you might withdraw, emotionally or physically, from me, so as to avoid getting stuck by my pin. As a result, we are not going to get very close.

I use this analogy to describe a pattern that often occurs in marriage. The "little irritations" in a relationship don't somehow magically go away. Instead, they infect the entire relationship, keeping the person who is being irritated constantly on edge.

Perhaps you are a person who prides yourself on not being irritated by little things. All day long, little things happen that irritate you, but they seem so petty that you keep your mouth shut. This may go on for a week or just a couple of days. The amount of time it goes on before you say something depends on many variables: stress, fatigue, consumption of alcohol, or any other variable that might affect a person's ability to control his or her emotions. After getting your fill of pinpricks or irritations, it takes just one small incident to trigger the emotional explosion. Usually the irritation that triggers you, if taken as an isolated incident, with all the other irritations, it is the proverbial "straw that broke the camel's back." When a person blows up in this way, other people may only see the incident that finally triggered the emotional reaction, and to them, the reaction seems far out of proportion to the incident that set the person off. People who lose their tempers in this fashion can be emotionally or even physically abusive to those around them, and because of this, they may be wrongly labeled as "hot-tempered."

Moreover, these experiences reinforce the hot-temper syndrome. People who perceive themselves as having a bad temper say to themselves, "Look what happens when I lose my temper. I could hurt somebody! I shouldn't let these little things bother me. I should work harder at controlling myself." But, of course, the more these people let their irritations accumulate, the more there is to explode when they get to the point that they can't stand anymore.

The way to break the pinprick pattern or the hot-temper syndrome is to acknowledge all those little irritations along the way, to verbalize your feelings. That way they won't accumulate in your system and burst forth in a destructive way. It's a lot easier to listen and resolve a problem when it's minor that to let it go until it has become a full-blown crisis.

To summarize, in thinking about these patterns, it is important not to *blame* yourself or your spouse. Most people are not aware of their behavioral patterns until an objective observer points them out. Even when they do become aware of a pattern, they might not know how to change or prevent it. One fortunate aspect to relationship patterns is that they recur again and again, with only the subject matter changing. So simply becoming aware of the common patterns described here will bring about change in your life. Don't be discouraged if, after recognizing your patterns and promising yourself to change, you find yourself falling back into old habits. Just keep reminding yourself of your pattern of behavior, and you'll be amazed to find that, after a few weeks of living with this awareness, your patterns really do change.

Part III
Sensuality and Intimacy

12. The Sexual Bond: Where Sensuality and Intimacy Become Creative Partners

Up to now, the main emphasis of this book has been on ways a couple can develop greater intimacy in their marriage. This intimacy in everyday life, in the common exchanges we all take so much for granted, is the foundation for sexual enjoyment in marriage. The more intimate the marriage partners become in their everyday exchanges outside the bedroom, the more mutually satisfying their sex lives will become.

All the topics discussed earlier in this book—neutrality, vulnerability, emotions, communication, and the resolution of conflicts—affect the quality of your sexual relationship. In this chapter, we'll see why this is true, and we'll explore how marriage partners can enhance their sexual relationship through increased awareness of the sexual myths, attitudes, and patterns that can trap people in an unsatisfactory sexual relationship.

Once again, the importance of awareness as the first step toward change cannot be emphasized too much. Just as we do not receive training on how to handle the other aspects of marriage, we are not taught what we can do to enjoy a satisfying sex life in marriage. The myth is that making love should happen "naturally." Why should you need to teach someone how to make love? But the truth is that fulfilling sexual interaction *must* be learned. The only aspect that may be instinctual is the mechanics of reproduction. It doesn't require mental and emotional intimacy to make a baby.

Most people learn sexual pleasure through trial and error, a process that can all too often lead to disappointment. Sex therapists, such as Masters and Johnson, suggest that at least half of all married couples experience at least some difficulties with sex, leaving much room for heightened pleasure in their relationship.

In these, the last pages of this book, we will talk about some of the things marriage partners can do not only to heighten sexual pleasure, but to allow sex to be the ultimate expression of their intimacy.

Becoming Aware of Typical Sexual Patterns

Just as there are common patterns in other aspects of marriage, so there are patterns in the sexual relationships of the people I see in my practice. To heighten our awareness of these patterns, let us take a look at an average couple.

The typical sexual pattern begins with the man making overtures to his wife. These are usually indirect and often nonverbal messages, such as a hug, a caress, or an embrace. Although the man usually initiates sex, both would like the initiation process to be more mutual. Usually the couple "saves" their sexual activity until the end of the day, after the children are asleep and the eleven o'clock news is over. By that time, both partners are tired and feeling anxious about getting to sleep so that they can get up in time for work the next day. Their senses are usually somewhat dulled by fatigue, limiting their capacity for pleasure, and they feel a certain amount of pressure to rush because they need their sleep, too. Foreplay generally lasts from five to ten minutes. Intercourse begins after the woman has reached what her husband considers to be a significant level of arousal. (And the good wife, remember, doesn't make her wants known.) The most common position for intercourse is with the man on top, often described as the "male superior" or "missionary" position. After the man ejaculates, the couple disengages and they kiss good-night. Sometimes the woman has an orgasm, sometimes she doesn't. But she expresses a rather passive view about this: "If it happens, that's fine. If it doesn't . . . well, maybe next time."

Learning about Each Other's Sexual Desires

According to the unspoken laws of the traditional marriage fantasy to which most of us unwittingly subscribe, the good husband is responsible for his wife's sexuality. What this means is that it is his job to see that she is satisfied. The degree to which he can satisfy her is a direct reflection of his masculinity and his ability as a lover. Some men come into my office saying, "Look, I've tried everything. I read *Joy of Sex* and even *More Joy of Sex*. I've touched her here, there, and everywhere, but nothing I do seems to work." He feels frustrated and inadequate about his ability to satisfy his wife's sexual needs.

What this man, along with many other good husbands, doesn't realize is that he is trying to do the impossible. Of course, he was well prepared for this responsibility through sex education in school. After all, didn't he take health education? Didn't he hear all those great stories in the locker room? And wasn't he an avid reader of *Playboy*? So he must know a lot about female sexuality, right? Wrong!

As for the wife's sexual background, her education about sexual pleasure went one of two ways. If she masturbated as a teenager and learned what pleased her, she probably didn't tell anyone. And she thinks she can't tell her husband now, because that might hurt his feelings and his ego. He might think that she's being too aggressive, or his image of her as a "nice girl" might be destroyed. On the other hand, she may have avoided her sexual feelings, waiting for the day when her husband would teach her all about sex. After all, he's a man and don't men know all about the subject?

Then we find this couple in bed together, full of great expectations for an exciting, satisfying sexual experience. What happens instead is that the husband tries to excite his wife by touching her, looking for that "right" place to touch that he read about in a book or heard described in a locker room conversation. He soon becomes frustrated, however, because his efforts don't have the desired effect. He's flying in a fog with no instruments to guide him. And while he fumbles, his wife also becomes frustrated. She may say to herself, "He doesn't seem to know what he's doing." Eventually, they both become so frustrated that they start to avoid the entire uncomfortable situation.

The only way a husband could possibly take responsibility for his wife's sexuality would be if the nerve endings of her body were wired to her husband's brain. Since this is not the case, there is little chance for the myth to become a reality.

But what if this couple dropped the traditional marriage fantasy and looked at sex another way. What if they followed the premise that *the husband is only responsible for his own sexuality and his wife is responsible for hers.* He is the best expert on what pleases him, and she is the only one who knows what pleases her—that is, until they give each other this information. Communicating your sexual wants or needs to your spouse is what taking responsibility for your sexuality means. Spouses need to teach each other about their bodies, to tell them and show them what they find pleasing.

The communication phrase "I want," which we have already discussed in other contexts, also applies to sex. When you use an *I* message, you are taking responsibility for yourself. When you tell your partner what you want sexually, you are telling him or her how to please you. This, in turn, pleases both partners, because both become secure in their ability to please the other.

In order to express what you want sexually, you have to know what turns you on. If you don't have this information, then you need to do some research. Such is the case of a woman who is preorgasmic—that is, a woman who has never experienced an orgasm, but has the natural potential to do so. This woman does not know what she needs to enjoy an orgasm. Since orgasm is usually easier to achieve alone than with another person, a woman can learn much about her sexual wants and needs by masturbating. Although masturbation may have been discouraged when we were children, it is now recognized as a perfectly acceptable and pleasurable activity, as well as an excellent way to gain self-knowledge about orgasm. As a preorgasmic woman learns what pleases her, she can communicate that information to her husband so that he will know what he should do to satisfy her wants or needs.

In the beginning of the courtship, some couples communicate their sexual wants or needs, but they may fail to update the information as their relationship progresses. A wife tells her husband, "I really like it when you touch me here," so every time they get together sexually he touches her in the same spot. After the second or third time, it may have stopped feeling good to the wife, but she doesn't tell him for fear of hurting his feelings. But, by not telling him, she may be hurting his feelings even more. Since he is no longer bringing her pleasure, she will probably lose interest in his lovemaking after a while. A person's wants change all the time, due to physiological changes, emotional moods, or physical energy levels. Therefore, it's important to keep your sexual partner up to date, so that you may have the chance to be sexually aroused and your partner may have the pleasure of seeing you that way.

As husbands confront the fact that they are not responsible for their wives' sexuality, many of them feel threatened, fearing that they will no longer be needed. But this is not the way it works. Letting go of that responsiblity means the husband does not have to perform a "job" or "duty" about which he knows little or nothing—his wife's sexuality. It is really only at this point that he can provide sexual pleasure for his wife. The only difference is that his wife is telling him exactly what he can do to maximize her sexual desires. Ultimately, her sexual pleasure will arouse him, deepening his own enjoyment and enhancing the couple's intimacy profoundly.

Goal-setting Dulls Pleasure

Another trap that couples may fall into after several years of marriage is goal-oriented sex. As Philip Slater points out in an essay called "Sexual Adequacy in America": "Our culture's obsession with achievement pervades our sexual lives. We strive to perfect the 'product,' orgasm, and ignore the pleasures of leisurely love."

A goal-oriented person focuses on the future instead of the present. It's like climbing a mountain and only focusing on getting to the top, without taking the time to smell the flowers or to check out the view along the way. "One who focuses only on the destination misses the pleasure of the journey," I often tell my clients.

The term *foreplay* demonstrates how completely goal-oriented sex has become entrenched in our thinking. *Foreplay*, of course, is the word we use to describe sexual activity prior to intercourse. It is not an end in itself, but one step in a series of steps whose purpose is to move toward a goal. You do this activity *before* you do something else. Most married couples engage in sexual foreplay with a purpose or goal in mind, to arouse themselves to the point where they can engage in sexual intercourse. It does not occur to them that foreplay is a pleasure in itself, one that can be enjoyed with or without intercourse and orgasm.

The goal-oriented nature of foreplay is reflected, also, in the fact that its duration shortens the longer a couple is married. When two people first begin having sexual relations, they usually spend most of their time touching, kissing, or petting. Whatever you call it—"making out," "necking," or "foreplay"—this activity is highly pleasurable and an important sexual activity. Depending on the couple, these activities might be brought to a climax in intercourse or the couple might be satisfied with the foreplay alone. This all seems to change once a couple gets married. Before they were married, they might have spent fifteen minutes touching and caressing each other, but after marriage they may spend five minutes. This five minutes is done with a "hurry-up-let's-get-through-it-so-we-can-*really*-get-it-on" kind of attitude. Thus, what was once a pleasurable activity that a couple spent quite a bit of time enjoying becomes just something to get through so they can get onto the real thing.

As the two people develop the attitude of sexual goal orientation—that is, foreplay for a purpose—their sexual relationship breaks down into a hierarchy of stages. Foreplay leads to intercourse, finally resulting in orgasm ($F \rightarrow I = O$). Once these stages become established, the couple's sexual relationship becomes rigid, predictable, and boring.

When you focus on the goal of orgasm, you focus on the future, and this limits or dulls your experience of the sexual stimulation you are receiving in the present. The intensity of your experience along the way becomes much diluted. A good example of how this becomes a problem can be seen in what happens with a woman who is striving very hard to have an orgasm. She's so busy worrying about whether or not she's going to have an orgasm that she misses the pleasure of the sexual stimulation that normally builds to that sensual peak.

Goal-oriented sex has another by-product: anxiety. Once you have a goal, you begin preparing yourself to achieve it. You begin thinking about how you must act, or perform, to achieve your goal. For example, a man may establish achieving an erection as the first part of his goal, so that he can "perform" the sex act. People who view sex as a performance are very likely to feel anxious. But anxiety and sexual pleasure do not go together. When your body is tight and controlled (as it would be in anticipation of a performance), rather than relaxed and open (as it would be in looking forward to experiencing pleasurable sensations), you are not able to feel much sexual pleasure. In other words, it's just damn difficult, if not impossible, to be turned on when you're feeling up-tight about performing sexually.

Another negative aspect of goal-oriented sex is the idea that all sexual interactions must lead to intercourse, to "going all the way." This idea, that once you get on the train, you've got to ride to the end of the line, is an unwritten rule for many couples. This rule affects a couple's sexual relationship in two important ways. First, it limits the couple's ability to have a flexible, changing sexual relationship. In his book, *Male Sexuality*, Bernie Zilbergeld describes a sexual myth that relates to this. The myth is: "Sex should be a process of continuously increasing excitement and passion. The sexual arousal must continue to build." He goes on to state that "because of this myth, the idea that sex can be leisurely, with breaks for resting, talking, laughing, or whatever, is foreign to many men." I would have to add that it is just as foreign to many women.

Flexibility, change, and unpredictability keep a long-term sexual relationship alive and exciting. For many couples, a sexual experience consists of a few minutes of foreplay, a few minutes of intercourse, all of which culminates in orgasm for the husband and, sometimes, for the wife. Time after time, they follow the same sequence. This is what I call "meat and potatoes sex." But who says sex has to be this way? Why can't there be a little touching, intercourse, back to touching, some intercourse, orgasm, and maybe some more touching, particularly if the woman was not fully satisfied through intercourse? By mixing up the usual sequence, numerous combinations can be created to keep the sexual experience varied, so it doesn't become just "the same old thing."

The unspoken rule that any sexual interaction must move on through all of its stages to orgasm discourages expression of affec-

tion on a more casual basis. Often I hear wives complain that if
they are affectionate with their husbands outside of the bedroom,
their husbands automatically jump to the conclusion that it's time
to make love. Both spouses end up assuming that physical affection must lead to sex. The result is that physical affection becomes
limited to a kiss when the two people see each other at the end of
the day. But why not expand this to a little petting and necking
with the mutual understanding that all this is an added luxury to
whatever other sexual activity you might want to enjoy at another
time of the day? Affection is a nonverbal way of expressing love
and caring in an intimate relationship. If this channel of communication is closed, the marriage partners have one less way of expressing their loving emotions for one another.

In the course of a day, it is not easy for a couple, particularly
when there are children around, to find time for intimate communication. If the two people have difficulty communicating verbally in an intimate way and, at the same time, are inhibited in communicating through physical affection, the lover aspect of their
relationship will quickly lose its intensity. Unless you nurture it
daily, this fragile part of your relationship is in jeopardy.

Somehow people expect that even though they don't communicate intimately throughout the day, they can have great sex when
they go into the bedroom after the eleven o'clock newscast. When
people don't communicate intimately throughout the day, they
put a heavy burden on their sexual relationship in the bedroom.
Indeed, far too many couples end up with sexual intercourse being their main way of expressing love. Those moments of love
stolen between the late-night news and sleep just aren't enough to
keep a relationship alive.

Not that there is anything wrong with intercourse as a way of
expressing love, but if it become the *only* way that two people
express their love for one another, it may collapse under the pressure. For many couples, it does. The pressure to "make" love can
turn the sexual experience from a pleasureful, sensual, relaxed,
enjoyable experience into a work-task-job, a goal- or product-ori-
ented experience. It is as though a little voice within us is saying,

"Marriages must have love, and now it's time to make some." No wonder the frequency of sex in most marriages declines with time. Who wants to work when you are ready to sleep at night, particularly if you have to be rested for the next day's work?

The reason many married people give for not initiating sex with their spouses is that they are tired. I often remind them of their pasts. When they were dating their spouses, how often did being tired or "having a headache" stand in the way of their engaging in sexual activity? And, believe me, neither age nor familiarity are causes of diminished sexual interest in their case. The problem lies in the fact that they have come to view sex as a performance or a job, which drains them of both mental and physical energy.

If married people could free themselves of goal-oriented sex and have a sexual relationship whose only purpose was mutual pleasure, they would quickly discover that familiarity leads to sex that is exciting, leisurely, and deeply satisfying. One does not grow bored with one's partner—one grows bored with the rigid structures imposed on a relationship. But that is something we can change. As pleasure increases, so will frequency. Instead of being a draining experience, sex will become a source of energy and relaxation.

Getting Free of Goals to Enjoy the Pleasures of the Moment

It is easy to say that goal orientation stands in the way of sexual pleasure, but we are a very goal-oriented society and this way of thinking has become a part of every one of us. All this is true. However, in recent years, psychologists have learned that there are simple mental techniques we can all use to renew our focus on bodily sensations that might otherwise be blocked by our thoughts. The following is the exercise that I've found to be most helpful for the couples with whom I work in my practice.

Preparation. Get into a comfortable position, either sitting in a chair with both your feet on the floor, hands resting gently on your knees, or lying on your back, hands at your sides and legs uncrossed. If you can do so, have a friend read the following instructions all the way through and become completely familiar with them before you start. You may then wish to keep this book beside you, with this exercise marked, so that you can easily refer to it as you go along.

Take your time. Do each part of this exercise in a slow and leisurely way.

Exercise: Close your eyes and let them stay closed until you finish this exercise. Now, turn your attention to the way your body feels. Say out loud the different things you feel inside your body. Be as specific as you can. For example, you might say, "I feel tension in my lower back," or "I feel the pulse in my right wrist." Say whatever you feel, describing whatever sensations you experience, no matter how insignificant they may seem to you.

As you become aware of the different feelings in your body, let yourself be aware of your environment. Describe your awareness. For example, you might say, "I'm aware of the traffic outside," or "I'm aware of the music in the next room." Take your time and explore your awareness of the environment, verbally describing your awareness.

Now, express out loud all the thoughts that you are thinking. Say out loud everything that crosses your mind, such as, "I'm thinking about eating dinner," or even "I'm thinking about thinking." Take your time. Explore and verbalize your thoughts in a leisurely way.

Turn your attention once more to what you feel in your body. Notice changes from the first time you focused on your body. Have parts that were once tense become relaxed? See if you can become aware of even the smallest of sensation, like maybe your glasses on your nose, your watch on your wrist, or your breathing.

Okay, now you can open your eyes.

Generally, when people go through this awareness experience, they feel much more relaxed than before they started. That's because they have acknowledged the messages that their bodies are sending them.

The point of this exercise is to allow you to explore the three types of conscious attention that can occur during sexual activity: (1) body feelings or sensations, (2) awareness of the environment, and (3) thoughts. We go in and out of these different levels of consciousness constantly, and the amount of time we spend in one or another can vary tremendously. Contrary to popular myth, we *do* have a choice about which consciousness mode we will be in at any given moment.

During sexual activity, if you are being touched and you're in the thinking mode, it will be difficult for you to feel the touch totally. And if, while being touched, you are aware of what your partner is doing, as if you were a spectator, or of activities in another room, it will also be difficult for you to enjoy the touching stimulation your partner is giving you. If, while you are being touched, you are into the body sensations mode, then you will feel the stimulation to its fullest. During sexual activity, the most pleasurable mode is the feeling or body sensations mode. You want to be aware of all the sensations you feel: warmth, coolness, the smooth or rough parts of the body, the texture of hair, and so forth. Too often couples overlook these sensations and only seek orgasm or "the big sexual turn-on." But here we are talking about sensuality, something that is missing in all too many couples' sexual relationships.

During sex with your mate, you may be focusing on your body feelings, but thoughts or an awareness of the environment may come into your consciousness and distract you. If this occurs, don't let it worry you. Simply acknowledge that awareness. As strange as this may sound, that is the best way to free yourself of them. Let yourself become aware of them—then let them go. Say hello to the thought or awareness of the environment, then let it slip through your mind, and say good-bye to it. Then go back to what you are feeling.

Some people find that small amounts of alcohol or marijuana help them focus on the feelings they have during sex. They describe themselves as being loose—more involved in the pleasure of the moment. The state of mind they describe is similar to the one people can achieve through the awareness exercise described above. While it is nice that these couples have found a way to enjoy their sexual experiences, it is unfortunate that people feel they must rely on drugs to help them to get into states of awareness they can achieve on their own.

In the process of becoming more sensitive to your own body, you become increasingly relaxed. This will not only help your sexual relationship, but it will carry over into all areas of your life. As one of my clients put it, "What a great thing to know I can relax myself any time I want."

How Often Is Enough?

Frequency of sexual activity, or lack of it, is a complex problem. In my practice as a marriage counselor, I find it to be the most common sexual problem. The causes are numerous, ranging from early childhood training to the temporary difficulties of the present relationship. One of the most common causes, difficulties with the present relationship, will be discussed here.

First, it is important to define what each person means by "sexual frequency." People often want to know how many times a week they should be having sex. The answer is that there are no set numbers. Each couple has its own needs, and so frequency standards are really determined only by the two partners. Frequency becomes an issue only when there is a great disparity between the partners' standards or needs. It is not unusual for one person to have a greater sex drive than the other, and this can become a source of tension both in and out of the bedroom. Stereotypically, it is the wife who makes up the excuses about why she isn't interested in sex. But, as with many stereotypes, this one is incorrect. I've seen as many men who don't require sex as often as their wives would like.

Infrequent sexual activity in marriage often reflects more on the quality of the experience than on biological drives. With couples who have a frequency problem, the quality or intensity of the sexual relationship is generally poor. The typical scenario goes like this: The husband is always wanting to make love. It appears that he has a high sex drive. Every time he and his wife go to bed, she feels pressured to meet his demands. In her mind, he is *always* ready to make love, and so she consents to making love, regardless of how she feels about it herself. So when this couple does have sex, there is considerable tension. Eventually, the husband senses his wife's hurry-up-and-get-it-over-with attitude. Even if she is a good actress at first, her act will wear thin with time. Sensing her tension, the husband never really relaxes and enjoys the sexual experience. Instead, he ejaculates, usually rapidly, with little touching preceding intercourse. With intercourse over, the couple kisses good-night, and the husband rolls over and goes to sleep. Frequently, the wife doesn't have an orgasm. The result is that while the husband has relieved his sexual tension, his wife has gotten little, if any, sexual satisfaction. This type of experience has been colloquially labeled "the quickie." Now, there is nothing wrong with a quickie once in a while, but a steady sexual diet of them can leave one sexually malnourished. This couple's sexual relationship is comparable to a steady diet of fast-food burgers. Eventually the diet will catch up to you.

After a number of years of this, a couple can get pretty turned off sex. Their sexual frequency drops off radically. In order to change this situation, this couple needs to discover quality. This will happen when the two people spend more time touching, more time caressing and being caressed, without having the pressure of needing to reach the goals of intercourse and orgasm every time. However, I can hear the wife in this relationship expressing a sigh of relief with that statement, and the husband saying, "What's sex without intercourse?"

To use the food metaphor once more, instead of going to the local fast-food chain for the usual quickie, we take this couple to an expensive French restaurant where they serve a five-course meal and every bite is worth savoring. Here the husband finds that his appetite is thoroughly satisfied. He's not so hungry the next night. His wife gets a little breathing room, and after a few "gourmet" encounters like this, she is able to assert herself sexually, initiating sexual contact as often as her husband. Now there is even more chance for her to get pleasure out of the sexual relationship.

One other cause for lack of sexual desire and frequency in a marital relationship is hurt, resentment, and anger buried away in either spouse. *It is very difficult to be sexually aroused by someone with whom you are angry.* We have already seen what happens to more generalized intimacy. Sexual desire is no different. It doesn't matter whether the repressed anger is over a small conflict that happened yesterday or is over something that has been building since the honeymoon ten years ago. If it gets repressed, the anger is going to affect that person's sexuality.

The expression of anger and the expression of sex are closely related physiologically. The actual expression of anger frees the expression of sexual feelings. Most couples have noticed how after an intense argument—one in which anger was freely expressed and a mutually satisfying resolution was achieved—they became sexually turned on to each other. The opposite is true when anger is controlled. Keeping anger down requires a great deal of emotional energy. And the more anger one feels, the more emotional energy he or she will need for its repression, if that's how the individual chooses to deal with it. After a number of years or hours repressing resentments or feelings of anger, the person becomes drained of sexual energy. Most couples who don't fight, and who pride themselves on how few conflicts they have, have emotionally flat sexual relationships.

Frigidity: Another Myth Exploded

Women who are not sexually responsive are often described as being "frigid." This label is misleading, confusing, and in my opinion, should be junked. The term *frigidity* is loosely applied to all forms of women's sexual inhibition, from total lack of erotic feelings to the occasional inability to reach orgasm. The causes of a woman's sexual inhibition are numerous and complex, but a term such as this one tries to lump all such causes together, giving the impression that frigidity is a single condition like measles or the common cold. Lack of sexual responsiveness is a *symptom*, not a cause, of marital conflict. A frigid woman is often assumed to be cold and distant with all men. This is simply not true. I find in my counseling practice that so-called frigid women are frequently affectionate people who are easily aroused, but who are inhibited by more general, usually nonsexual, conflicts in their relationships.

I find that women who perceive themselves as frigid are angry people. They are angry about things that their husbands have done or said. They are angry about feeling that they have lost too often in too many conflicts in their marriages. They may be angry at the conditions of their lives. Usually this anger is related to a lack of self-esteem and self-development, and it may be well-hidden and repressed.

In the early years of her marriage, such a woman may have felt it was unsafe to communicate her opinions or express her anger, so all of it got repressed. She built an impenetrable wall around her anger so it wouldn't upset her marriage. As the years went by, she collected more and more anger and resentment, and she found that she had to build the protective wall larger and thicker. Like a nuclear reactor, she has a "hot core," but instead of radioactive plutonium, it is a hot core of anger. Just as the outer walls of a reactor are cool, so too is a "frigid" woman's emotional exterior. A frigid woman may *appear* unemotional, but inside there is that seething hot core of resentment that she believes she must contain. She is afraid that if even a small crack develops in that wall, her anger will blast it apart and the resulting explosion will destroy her marriage. The problem is that while she represses her anger, she also represses her sexual feelings.

The same process by which she seeks to maintain her marriage ultimately triggers a crisis that threatens its very existence. If she were able to express the anger she thinks she needs to repress, she could begin to change things for the better. Her fear keeps her paralyzed, however, and it is as though she is afraid that anything she does, anything at all, will not only "rock the boat," but swamp it. Of course, there is always a risk involved in change, but if this woman does not change, she will probably drive her husband into an extramarital affair or even the divorce courts. Unless she risks change, she will lose the very thing she is trying to preserve.

The label *frigidity* is applied to women, but what do you call a man who expresses little sexual desire or interest? In my practice, I see just as many men as women who have low sexual desire. These husbands cannot understand why they don't have much sexual interest in their wives. A husband will say that he loves his wife and is still attracted to her, but that he just seems to have lost his sexual appetite. Then I ask him what he does when his wife hurts his feelings or makes him angry. The most common answer I hear from the frigid male is that he "controls" his anger or hurt. Sound familiar? He, too, builds a psychological wall around his pain, anger, and all the rest of his emotions. He appears to be a nice guy, even warm and affectionate, but when it comes to sexual interaction, he freezes up.

Now, of course, there could be other psychological or maybe physical reasons for a person's lack of sexual desire, but the repression of hurt and anger is far and away the most common cause. Again, it is very hard to be sexually responsive to someone that you are angry with, whether that anger is old or new, little or big. If it hasn't been effectively communicated and acknowledged, that anger is going to inhibit the free-flowing expression of sexual desire from that individual.

Time and again, men tell me they can't stand to be nagged at or bitched at by their wives. They want to be left alone unless the problem is major and worth their time. The expression of this attitude sounds like this: "Will you quit bugging me? I have a lot on my mind," or "You are always bitching about something. So what if I do this or that? Those are such little things. You can't let the little things bug you so much." This husband is telling his wife to repress, rather than communicate, the things that bother her. If he only knew how this attitude affects his wife's sexual response, he might be more willing to listen to her. Most men don't fully understand how this attitude affects their wives and cripples their sex life until the whole matter reaches a crisis point, and by that time it may be too late.

Just as two may *cause* frigidity, it takes two to work out a solution. For example, the husband of a so-called frigid wife could decide to listen to her when she tries to tell him what bothers her. He could encourage her to communicate all the little things that make her mad so that she won't store up her resentments. With the emotional channels open, there is nothing blocking the full expression of her sexual desires and feelings. Of course, the same thing goes for the wife whose husband is frigid. Encouraging the other person to keep communication open benefits both partners. It is amazing how quickly "frigid" mates become sexually responsive when they learn to communicate their feelings to their partners. The process requires patience on the part of both husband and wife, but the eventual benefits are well worth it.

Initiation: Who Does What When?

The marriage fantasy includes socially reinforced rules about who should initiate sex, and these rules can become a real source of conflict in marriage. The basic rule of the fantasy is that men should be sexually aggressive and frank about their erotic feelings, while women should be sexually passive and at least quiet about their erotic feelings. During adolescence, even the language of sexuality expresses these differences: the boy tries to "score," while the girl tries not to be "too easy."

Negative stereotyping is the punishment for anyone who deviates from these rules. If a girl becomes too sexually aggressive, she risks being labeled a whore, a slut, or a "bad girl." If a boy is sexually passive, he isn't a man, or he is considered shy or a "chicken." Here are the roots of our society's double standards.

The idea that a woman should be sexually passive and a man should be aggressive is, of course, carried into marriage. These sexist roles generate rigidity in a couple's sexual relationship. A man and woman may be comfortable with the stereotypical roles when they first get married, but after a while they are both going to feel a bit stifled. He is going to become tired of always being the one who has to initiate sex. He may even start to wonder whether his wife is attracted to him sexually. Meanwhile, the wife may become tired of always waiting for her husband to make the first move. She would like to feel free to express her sexuality whenever she feels like it, without having to worry that her actions are going to affect her husband's opinion of her adversely.

In a questionnaire I give to couples I see for counseling, I ask which partner initiates sex in the marriage and what changes, if any, they would like in this. Most people answer that the husband initiates sex, but, interestingly enough, both partners state that they would prefer it if sexual initiation was more equal.

One common problem that compounds this whole issue of initiation is that spouses often have difficulty communicating their sexual desires. Consider the following verbal exchange: John says,

"I think I'll take a shower." What that really means is, "I'm going to clean up for you so we can make love." Linda replies, "I'll be there in a few minutes." This means yes to making love. Or she may reply, "I have a headache," which means no to any sexual activity. People rarely say to their mates, "I'd really like to have sex with you tonight." Instead, they develop a whole language of innuendo to communicate their sexual wants or needs.

With any language of this kind, there is a great deal of room for misunderstanding. Most married couples find sexual initiation to be an emotionally loaded issue at best, and under these circumstances, it is no wonder that people's feeling get hurt. For example, John may announce he's going to take a shower and go to bed, anticipating that Linda will join him. After fifteen or twenty minutes, she still doesn't come, and he begins to wonder if she's rejecting his advances. Half an hour later, she still hasn't arrived, and by now he's really angry. He gets on his bathrobe and goes into the living room to find her deeply engrossed in the late-night movie. He blows up at her, accusing her of avoiding him—while the truth is that when he announced that he was taking a shower and going to bed, she didn't recognize it as a sexual advance.

In addition to leaving a great deal of room for misunderstanding, a language of innuendo also sets up a couple for a ritualized pattern in their sex life. They may pick one particular night each week to be sexual so they don't have to risk ambiguity, rejection, or misunderstanding each time. Not much effort is required with this arrangement, but under these circumstances, sex becomes predictable and boring.

I would like to offer a more constructive and open approach to initiating sex in marriage. The first step is to acknowledge to each other that both of you have sexual feelings. It is normal and healthy to have these feelings whether you are male or female. To fully acknowledge this reality, it is important to give each other permission to be the initiator. Talk over this issue with your mate. Be explicit. You'll probably discover that your partner would also like more flexibility in who initiates sex.

The second step in reducing initiation conflicts involves the communication process itself. Instead of using a language of innuendo, be verbally explicit. Tell your mate that you would like to have sex with him or her. Learn to communicate your sexual needs as clearly as you would express that you're hungry, or would like to go to a show, or would like to get away for a vacation. Instead of saying, "I'm going to take a shower now," as John did in the example above, say what you really mean: "I'd like to have sex with you tonight." This may not be easy at first, but as you develop your way of asking in your own style, it will begin to feel natural and easy.

Similarly, learn to say no when you really mean no.

Most people can't tell how much they really want sex at any given moment. They fall somewhere between the extremes of "definitely not now" and "absolutely yes." When you feel ambivalent or neutral, lend yourself to the experience. Let us explore that a bit.

Often people come home from work with everything but sex on their minds. They may be immediately confronted by partners who want to engage in sexual activity right away. If they respond on the basis of how they feel at that moment, they probably refuse. However, if they consider *lending themselves to the experience,* going along with their partner's sexual desires even though at the moment they are not interested in sex, what they may find is that they become quite aroused after a while.

What if this person is still neutral after a period of time? That would be okay, because he or she would still be able to hold and touch his or her spouse and be affectionate. What blocks people from lending themselves to the sexual experience is the rule that "once you start any form of sexual activity, it must culminate with intercourse." If a person is not sure that he or she wants to have intercourse, that person tends to refrain from almost any physical contact, and this does not have to be. Give each other permission to be affectionate without intercourse and you will greatly increase your pleasure in affectionate touching and physical contact.

Many married people become afraid of initiating any sexual activity because they fear being turned down or rejected by their spouses. A lot of people, particularly men, get their feelings hurt or their sexual self-images damaged by this rejection. One author put it this way:

Being turned down for sex, even in marriage, is a bump to the ego—in part because that is how we felt before marriage, and in part because in marriage it is a right. To protect ourselves we wait for the other person to make the first move. This is particularly anxiety-provoking for men, because it is they who are usually expected to make the first move, and who run the risk of being turned down. At the same time many men have difficulty letting their wives take the initiative.

Suppose the person who wants to make love says so in a very direct way? If a husband says to his wife, "I would like to make love tonight," he is stating a clear desire. That is *his* agenda for their time together. But perhaps his wife responds by saying, "That sounds nice, but I want to go to sleep early tonight." She, too, is clearly stating *her* agenda for the evening. It just happens that her agenda is in conflict with her husband's.

Typically, what happens when this conflict occurs is that the person who initiated feels rejected and hurt, but is this person being rejected or is this person being disappointed because his or her agenda cannot be carried out? Most often, it is disappointment. When a spouse says no to sex, he or she is probably *not* telling the partner, "You are a lousy lover," or "You're unattractive," or "Get out of my life." Instead, he or she is saying, "Not now. I'm not in the mood, but I still find you sexually attractive." This is the difference between being disappointed and being rejected. Remember, just because a spouse says he or she wants something doesn't mean he or she has to get it.

To reduce any anxiety you may feel when your partner turns you down, ask yourself this question, "Am I mad because I'm being rejected, or am I upset because I'm disappointed?" More often than not, you will come to the conclusion that it's the latter. As you learn to distinguish between rejection and disappointment, you will find that your fear of rejection will fade, and without this fear, you will become more comfortable about initiating sex.

Creating Romantic Settings

When a couple is courting or dating, they spend a great deal of

---

*John Gagnon, *Human Sexualities* (Glenview, Calif.: Scott Foresman, 1977), p. 209.

time and energy making themselves and their cars or living quarters attractive. They may wash and polish their cars, vacuum their apartments, spend an hour in front of the mirror putting on make-up, and another hour selecting the right kind of music for the stereo. They take great care to "set the scene." The goal is to create a sensuous mood. Everything is aimed at enhancing the pleasure of their time together.

After marriage, people usually stop putting out the effort to create a sensuous atmosphere. It is almost as though, having played the seduction game and won their conquest, they feel they can kick back and take it easy "until death do us part." This kind of complacency robs a relationship of its vitality and may even lead to its demise, because it does not acknowledge people's continuing need for attractive and sensuous surroundings.

Married people can re-energize their sexual relationships by creating an atmosphere that is pleasurable. Don't do it with the goal of seducing your mate, but as a way of creating pleasure, in and of itself, for both of you. Pleasure in the way you feel and in the way you look to your mate, as well as the pleasure you and your mate feel in your surroundings, fosters pleasure in intimacy and sex.

Is Spontaneity Natural?

Another attitude that makes initiation difficult is the belief that sexual activity should always be spontaneous. People who subscribe to this belief insist that sex should never require thought or planning. They would say that if you're hungry, you eat—if you feel "horny," you have sex. As Bernie Zilbergeld points out in his book, *Male Sexuality*, people act as if "there should be no necessity for learning any skills, talking about sex, or taking any corrective measures, for there is nothing to learn and nothing to correct." Sex probably would be more natural and spontaneous if it wasn't for the fact that when we were children, we learned rules, restriction, beliefs, parental attitudes, and societal standards that make it difficult for most of us to express our "natural" desires freely.

Considering the lifestyles of today, it is obvious that there are far too many distractions—shopping, caring for the children, civic responsibilities, and work—which, even from the point of view of logistics, greatly hamper sexual spontaneity. The idea that " sex should just happen any time" might be okay if you and your partner were living by yourselves in the wilderness, but even there one would have to structure one's time for gathering or cultivation, maintaining a house or other shelter, and so forth.

I often ask couples who have come to me for counseling, "Now that you have been married for a number of years and the novelty and excitement of being together has worn off, what motivates you to initiate sex?" Of course, there are many answers to this question, but a common theme weaves through them all: In the beginning of a relationship, people initiate sex in response to their attraction to their mates and to the excitement of being with a new person. They get *turned on* by each other very easily. Just seeing the other person naked is exciting enough to motivate a sexual advance. But what happens after a few years, when the partners have become familiar with each other and the automatic attractions that once aroused and motivated them to initiate sex are gone? All too many people become confused at this point and may even feel that they no longer love their partners because this *visual* attraction and the *mystery* or *romance* seems to have waned. Some people get stuck at this stage of relationship development, while others quickly discover what lies beyond—pleasure in knowing how to give and receive pleasure with a person who can fully reciprocate.

An Exercise to Explore Pleasure

So far in this chapter we have discussed some of the common problems that reduce sexual pleasure in marriage, and I have offered some solutions that have helped many couples in my practice. As we have seen, intimacy occurs on many levels in marriage, but all the benefits come together in a very special way with sex. In the following paragraphs, I will describe a structured sexual experience that I often assign to the couples with whom I work. It is a way to bring together everything discussed in this book, using sensual experience as a focus.

I suggest that both partners read this entire book, of course, but it is especially important that both read this exercise. The reasons will become obvious as we go along.

I suggest that the person who ordinarily initiates sexual activity in the marriage be the one to start. If both partners initiate, more or less equally, then it is not important who begins.

I suggest that the partner who starts this experience begin with an *I* message, stating that he or she would like to do this exercise. If the other partner responds positively, then the couple has mutually agreed. If the other partner responds negatively, then both should wait until there is mutual agreement. The key is mutuality. Do not do this experience unless both of you want to. Otherwise, no lasting change will take place.

Once mutuality has been established, the initiating partner takes responsibility for creating an atmosphere that will enhance the comfort and sensuality of both partners. This might include setting the temperature of the room, making the room attractive, seeing that the kids (if any) aren't going to interrupt, and so forth.

Both partners should be naked, of course. The partner initiating this experience—let's say it's the wife—starts by touching her husband wherever she wants. The only place she cannot touch, throughout this exercise, is the genital area. As she moves her hands over her husband's body, she has no goal. She is touching for her own pleasure and information. She is not trying to turn him on. She is not trying to give him an erection or an orgasm. This touching is all for her. Let her focus be on what she feels as she touches her husband. She should move all thoughts about what her husband is thinking or feeling—about the kids, about the long day tomorrow, about whatever else—out of her mind. She can pretend that the nerve endings are wired to an amplifier. She turns up the volume. She takes her time to be aware of all the little sensations she receives, everything she feels—the smooth or rough areas, the cool and warm parts, the places that are dry or damp or hairy. She will be looking for the subtle, sensual feelings rather than for some big sensation.

She can touch her husband as long as she wants, so long as it is comfortable for him. But this experience should last more than a few minutes. The touching may seem uncomfortable at first, but she should continue until she has become relaxed with it. Her husband, the receiver of her touch, is only responsible for communicating to his wife nonverbally by moving her hand to a neutral part on his body, if a place she is touching doesn't feel good to him. If she can trust that her husband will take care of himself in this way, she won't have to worry while she is touching him. She won't have to say to herself, "I wonder if he likes this," or "I hope I'm not tickling him." She can assume that if he is not moving her hand, then wherever she touches is fine with him. If she doesn't have to take care of her husband by worrying about him sexually, she will be free to indulge and experience her own pleasurable sensations.

By spending all this time discussing the pleasure that the initiator is feeling, I don't mean to imply that the other person—in this case, the husband—is not supposed to enjoy the sensations he is experiencing.

When the wife is done touching her husband, the situation is reversed. Now he touches her and she receives. As before, he is touching his wife for his own pleasure and information. He isn't trying to turn her on or give her an orgasm. He is to touch her from her head to her toes with the exception of her breasts and genitals. The same agreement is made that if he touches her in a way or in a place that doesn't feel good to her, she is to move his hand quietly to another place. Trusting that she will take care of herself in this way, the husband is free of worry and can indulge in his own sensations of pleasure.

This sexual experience has no goal except the mutual pleasure of those involved. It is not "foreplay." It is sex. This experience, done in this structured manner, *is not meant to lead to sexual intercourse.* Through this sexual experience of touching, the couple is learning to be sexual apart from intercourse and orgasm. I want them to experience each other sexually without the pressure that once they start touching, they have to "go all the way."

After a couple has finished this experience, I want them to repeat the experience within the next couple of days. But this time the partner who initiated the experience the first time becomes the receiver. This time there are no restrictions on where the partners touch each other. Breasts and genitals can be touched. But don't forget that the point of this exercise is to experience the subtler pleasures of sex. Continue to touch the whole body and just include the genitals and breasts. Also, unlike the first experience, the receiver can now move the toucher's hand to show nonverbally where touching feels particularly good. This does not mean that the toucher is no longer touching for his or her own pleasure. If he or she doesn't want to touch in the way that the receiver is showing, then he or she doesn't have to. But most partners feel good when they are pleasing their partners sexually. Just as in the first time around, this exercise should not culminate with intercourse. If one or both partners have an orgasm while they're being touched, that's fine, but having an orgasm is not the goal.

Both parts of this structured sexual experience are to be done without a goal. The pleasure of each moment is the focus. These experiences are not to lead to intercourse. Each spouse is touching for his or her own pleasure, rather than touching to arouse the partner—even though this may be a secondary benefit. All communication should be nonverbal. Don't make comments like, "Oh, that feels great" or "Touch like that." Talking leads to thinking, rather than feeling.

This two-part sexual experience promotes several attitudes that enhance a sexual relationship. The first is the idea of "selfishness." These experiences are designed to shift a partner's goal from trying to arouse his or her partner sexually to touching for his or her own pleasure. This might sound like a shift from giving pleasure to being selfish. In her book, *The New Sex Therapy*, Helen Kaplan Singer states that, during sex therapy, "it is often essential to teach the couple the value of temporary *selfishness* so that they can lose themselves to the sexual experience." She also states that "to function well sexually, the individual(s) must be able to abandon themselves to the erotic experience." They must be able to give up control and some degree of contact with their environment temporarily.

Too often during a sexual encounter, the partners are so busy trying to please and arouse one another that they pay no attention to the pleasure they themselves are receiving. As a result, they inadvertently frustrate each other's efforts. These experiences help people learn to receive and give pleasure, which may be difficult for some, but essential to a satisfying, sexual experience.

This whole idea of "selfishness" in sex deserves a closer look. If a husband is touching his wife for his own pleasure, if he is really enjoying what he is doing and isn't hurting or irritating his wife, then I would think that his wife would be deriving pleasure from the fact that he is enjoying what he is doing to her sexually. It may actually be "selfish" for him not to enjoy himself. If she senses that he's "just doing his job" and is not particularly enjoying what he's doing, it will be difficult for his wife to enjoy herself. She is going to be *thinking* so much about her husband that she will feel very few pleasurable sensation. When you do what feels good to you, you allow your partner to experience his or her own pleasure.

In the second sexual touching experience, where genitals are included as a touchable area, each partner is learning to take responsibility for his or her own sexuality. Each partner teaches the other, through nonverbal communication, ways to enhance his or her own sexual pleasure through genital touching. They are giving each other the knowledge of how and where they like to be touched, reducing the level of frustration involved in their sexual relationship and increasing the amount of pleasure both feel.

These experiences also teach a person that his or her whole body is one big erogenous zone. Partners whose sexual relationship is of the "meat and potatoes" variety, focus all their attention on very limited areas of each other's bodies. For the man, his genitals, and for the woman, her breasts and genitals. This couple overlooks all the other body areas that offer sensual pleasure. Touching these other areas of the body, such as ears, neck, or feet, may not directly lead to an erection or orgasm, but will provide much sensual pleasure.

As John Gagnon points out in his book, *Human Sexualities*, "What makes zones of the body erotic or sexual is the context in which they are touched and the meanings that are attributed to that touching." There are no special nerve endings that induce sexual arousal. The nerve endings that are located in our genitals are the same kinds of nerve endings as those located in our hands or feet. The only difference between them is in the number of nerve endings and the meanings we apply to these areas. For example, there is no automatic, physiological connection between a woman's breasts and the blood flow into a male's genitals. A man learns through his socialization process that this is a sexual event. If he had grown up in a society where a woman's ears were considered a highly erogenous zone, he might become sexually aroused when he saw or touched them. In some cultures, women's breasts are exposed all the time and are not considered to be a particularly erotic zone.

So keep in mind, if you will, that the touching exercise described here is meant to educate you about the nerve endings all over the body and to help you become aware of their varying degrees of sensitivity. Given a sexual, intimate, or loving context, all areas of the body may provide sensual-sexual excitement. Many people are looking so hard for *the right place* that will provide the "big turn-on" that they miss all the sensuous, pleasurable sensations along the way. The level of *sensuality* is what makes and keeps a long-term sexual relationship satisfying.

Orgasm: Are There Right and Wrong Ways to Achieve It?

Volumes have been written on the subject of orgasm, some of them helpful and some of them downright quackery. The most frequently repeated myth in these discussions is that a woman should have an orgasm during intercourse and that any other form of stimulation is either inadequate or unnatural. If one were to believe everything that has been written and said on the subject, he would jump to the conclusion that a woman's sexual adequacy is determined by how rapidly she can achieve orgasm *during intercourse*.

The emphasis on intercourse as the proper way for a woman to achieve orgasm had its beginnings with Freud. He divided women's orgasms into two types. He called one type "clitoral" and referred to it as infantile and appropriate during childhood. The second type he called "vaginal," and this was, to his way of thinking, a more mature form of orgasm that occurred during or after puberty. From the traditional psychoanalytic point of view, a woman must make the transition from the clitoral to the vaginal type of orgasm before she can be considered to have achieved appropriate psycho-sexual development. Commenting on this myth in his essay, "Sexual Adequacy in America," Philip Slater states that "before Masters and Johnson undermined the dogma of vaginal orgasm, two generations of women had felt guilty and inadequate because of a man's fantasy about how their bodies should function."

It wasn't until Masters and Johnson did their historic research that the dichotomy between clitoral and vaginal orgasm was shown to be a false one. There is only one kind of female orgasm. It is physiologically triggered through either direct or indirect stimulation of the clitoris. Masters and Johnson have aptly defined the function of the clitoris as the "transmitter and conductor of erotic sensation."

Even though these physiological truths have been known for a long time now, and have been completely accepted by the medical and psychological community, the myth still persists with the general public. But if Masters and Johnson are right, and Freud's view of female orgasm is no longer accepted, then what is the *right* way for a woman to have an orgasm? The answer is quite simple: any form of stimulation that carries a woman to the point of orgasm is normal and right for her. When a man and woman understand and accept this, they will probably enjoy greater freedom and flexibility in their sexual relationship right away. The husband will no longer need to place so much importance on his ability to use his penis and to control his speed of ejaculation, and both partners will be free to explore other methods of stimulation. Considering the number of problems a man creates for himself when he feels that he must prove himself capable of stimulating his wife to the point of orgasm using only his penis, the new view of female orgasm proves to be as liberating for him as for her.

For so many couples, sexual activity is finished when the husband has had his orgasm or ejaculation. If the woman has had an orgasm also and is satisfied at this point, that's fine. But for many women, intercourse alone does not provide enough clitoral stimulation for them to reach an orgasm. Thus, they are left unsatisfied. Many women say they are satisfied just being touched and held.

But my experiences with couples in counseling lead me to believe such women are often feeling inadequate or even guilty about not having an orgasm and are trying to make themselves and their partners feel all right about its absence. In therapy, we discover that when these women and their partners learn to accept oral or manual stimulation, they become more assertive about achieving orgasm.

The focus on female orgasm has played a major role in the sexual revolution of the past couple of decades. It has become the measure by which men judge their sexual performance and ability. "Did you come?" "Was it good?" "How many times did you come?" These questions reflect the man's need for sexual validity and approval. Not that having orgasms is bad per se. But when so much emphasis is placed on the man's ability to *cause* his partner to have orgasms, pleasure is pushed into the background and sexuality becomes a competitive game scored by the total number of orgasms attained.

As Philip Slater pointed out, "Discussions of sexuality in America have always centered on orgasm rather than on pleasure in general." Again, this is a reflection of our cultural tendency to be more concerned with attaining our goals than with the pleasure in the activity experienced along with way to that goal. Although women are becoming increasingly goal-oriented in our society, it is still a value that more men than women hold. When, for example, a man asks his sexual partner if she has had an orgasm, he asks not so much because he is concerned with her pleasure, but because he is keeping score on himself. The bigger the orgasm she has, or the greater number she achieves, the better the man's sexual performance or the more successful he was at his *sexual task*. I point this out not for the sake of ridiculing the man's misalliance of priorities—for, after all, it is part of the marriage fantasy taught to men and women alike—but to help men become aware of one way in which they limit their own pleasure.

It is important for couples to be satisfied with their orgasms, but to be aware also of how orgasm as a goal can be a trap. Making orgasm the be-all and end-all of sexual activity is as limiting as denying the person the right to have an orgasm. The experience of orgasm is not a guarantee of sexual pleasure. Sexual pleasure is greatly enhanced when couples shift their attention from orgasm to the sensual pleasures that can be enjoyed on the way to having an orgasm. One can achieve orgasm without being fully aware of the pleasures leading up to it. However, when a couple learns to enjoy the sensual experience along the way, that process not only flows naturally into orgasm, but results in sexual fulfillment previously undreamed of by either partner.

Exercise No. 4: Sexual *I* Messages

(Note the similarities between this exercise and Exercise No. 2. Here the exercise is applied specifically to sexuality.)

PURPOSE: To develop skills in communicating sexual wants in your relationship.

PREPARATION: Arrange approximately one full hour when you and your spouse can be together without interruptions and without distractions. Both partners review this chapter before sitting down together to do this exercise.

EXERCISE: Sit facing each other. You will be taking turns expressing and listening. If you are the listener, do not interrupt your mate except to ask for clarification. While doing this exercise, do not argue, debate, or discuss anything being expressed. Listen as an objective third person.

When you are expressing your wants, begin each statement with the pronoun *I*. Express each of the following to your mate:

1) *Appreciation:* Tell your mate one thing you appreciate about him or her, as it applies to your sexual relationship. Tell him or her a single thing about his or her personality or behavior that turns you on sexually. Be clear about your feelings and express yourself using the *I* pronoun.

2) *Resentment:* Tell your mate about a single aspect of his or her personality or behavior that turns you off sexually. Be specific, clear, and brief. Begin each statement with *I*.

3) *Want or Need:* Tell your mate about a single thing you want or need from him or her in your sexual relationship. Be very clear. Describe a specific action he or she can take.

Reverse roles so that the speaker becomes the listener and the listener becomes the speaker.

You may repeat this exercise as many times as you wish, trading back and forth, taking turns as listener and speaker.

After both partners have completed this exercise, do not further discuss the issues raised here. Although you may have strong feelings about some of the information communicated, bear in mind that you are not *required* to do anything about it, nor should you expect your mate to change something in his or her behavior immediately because of what you have expressed here. You are not being ordered to change, in the way that your parents or teachers may have ordered you when you were a child, nor are you assuming a parental role and ordering your spouse to change. Instead, you are exchanging information about what you and your mate feel you want from each other. What you finally choose to do with this information is entirely up to you.

Remember that asking does not guarantee you will get what you want. It only *informs* others of your wants. Similarly, when others inform you of what they want, you are not obligated to fulfill their wants. There are no guarantees in life.

Exercise No. 5: Blind Walk

PURPOSE: As has been discussed in previous chapters, the basic psychological components for a satisfying marital-sexual experience are a high degree of trust and vulnerability between partners and an ability to focus on nonvisual sensual experience. This exercise provides a couple with a structured way to enhance these qualities within their relationship.

PREPARATION: Set aside thirty minutes or more, perhaps in the evening after supper, when you and your mate can take a long walk together.

EXERCISE: While holding hands, play "blind man" as you may have done when you were a child. One person closes his or her eyes while the other leads, giving instructions, when necessary, to step up or down curbs, to step around an obstacle, and so forth.

While you are being led in this way, focus your attention on smells, sounds, and the feeling of the ground under your feet. If you are anxious about not being able to see where you are going, keep your eyes closed, but communicate your anxiety to your mate. If you feel reluctant to trust yourself in your mate's hands, discuss that with them as well.

After ten minutes or more, reverse roles. Again, discuss any anxiety or reluctance to trust the person who is leading you.

When you finish this exercise, discuss those things you may have noticed more than usual sounds, scents, and feelings while you were being guided along by your mate.

Part IV
Conclusion

13. Can This Book Really Help?

Now that you have read this book, I want to pose a question that many people in my profession, as well as our clients, ask again and again. Can books of this kind really help to change and improve a marriage which is uncomfortable or which just plain isn't working? And, for that matter, can the many available workshops and classes on inner growth really help? Can long-term therapy help? Frankly, the answer to all of these questions is no. Neither books nor classes nor workshops nor therapy per se can help. But *awareness* can help. For only if we are aware of how we are now and what we might do to improve our lives can we even speculate on change. And this awareness can come through any vehicle of communication, from long-term therapy to something as seemingly insignificant as a few lines in a book. Words are indeed powerful, possessing great energy for triggering change, but the awareness that words provide us is only a beginning, the first step toward change.

More often than not, the people who come to me for help are *aware* of why their marriages are unhappy. Many can make long, clearly articulated lists of the reasons their relationships are failing. They are *aware*—yet they resist change. Why? Why don't they either divorce their mates or start working to improve their relationships? One word—*motivation*—tells the whole story. Unfortunately, most of us aren't truly motivated to change until the pain of staying the way we are outweighs the discomfort we anticipate at the prospect of change. It takes a lot of energy and courage to change. It especially takes a lot of energy to make the first assertive moves toward change. It is like trying to get a huge, overloaded wagon rolling once again after its wheels have sunk into the earth. Getting it rolling—that is, overcoming the inertia—will call upon all your resources. Once you're rolling, it gets easier, but *starting* that forward motion requires more energy than most of us are accustomed to putting out.

Many people, especially women caught up in the traditional marriage fantasy, fear change because there are no guarantees that the change will work. And husbands may be so threatened by their wives' demands that things will actually get much worse before they get better. The wife who faces such a prospect will also have to face the prospect of losing financial security. And, though it sounds contradictory, she may have to give up emotional security as well. There is, after all, security in that which is familiar, even when it is painful. As creatures of habit, we tend to shun the unknown, even when it promises improvement in our lives. The motivation to change comes only when a person can say, "I don't care what's out there, I am no longer going to stand for things the way they are."

In addition to *awareness* and *motivation*, there is a third element necessary for change: *acceptance*. Whenever a marriage has become so difficult that the couple is actively seeking help to change the relationship, tension is high and each partner has a tendency to want to blame the other. It is as though each person is saying, "Everything would be all right if only you would do such and such." It is always easier to see the faults of others before we see our own. And how much easier life would be if others would change to accommodate me, rather than me changing to accommodate them!"

Before change can occur in a marriage, all blame must cease. To stop this blaming pattern, both partners must accept the fact that, except in very rare circumstances, both husband and wife participate in creating marital conflict. It is a fact of life that when the emotional balance sheets are objectively tallied, husband and wife have equal scores. Start with that knowledge. Don't get into the blame game, a game that no one ever wins. At any given time, the person who is getting blamed will feel rejected and, instead of changing, will resist and withdraw or become defensive and launch a counterattack. The counterattack gains nothing, except that now *both* partners feel rejected.

Blaming oneself for past errors doesn't help matters either. Instead of blaming yourself for past mistakes, give yourself credit for recognizing them. Then take it easy. Learn from your own history so that you don't have to repeat old patterns.

Accepting your spouse (or yourself) doesn't mean that you must approve or disapprove, like or dislike, everything they do or have done. Just accept the reality that these things have happened or are happening, and start talking about how you can change them for the better. Without acceptance, there can be no change.

In summary, the three elements necessary for change are: *awareness*, *motivation*, and *acceptance*. All the book knowledge in the world, all the workshops and therapy won't help unless these three elements are present—and that depends on you.

Human beings grow and change all through their lives, and as long as we can allow ourselves to learn new things, the hope for improvement in our lives goes on. Knowing that we *can* change and then *wanting* to do it—these are the first two big steps toward enjoying greater intimacy in our marriages and ultimately improving the emotional quality of our lives.

Bibliography

Alberti, Robert, and Emmons, Michael. *Your Perfect Right: A Guide to Assertive Behavior.* San Luis Obispo, Calif.: Impact Publishers, 1970.

Bach, George, and Goldberg, Herb. *Creative Aggression.* Garden City, N.Y.: Doubleday & Co., 1974.

Bach, George, and Wyden, Peter. *The Intimate Enemy: How to Fight Fair in Love and Marriage.* New York: William Morrow Co., 1968.

Bandler, Richard, Grinder, John, and Satir, Virginia. *Changing with Families.* Palo Alto, Calif.: Science and Behavior Books, Inc., 1976.

Bird, Carolyn. *The Two Paycheck Marriage.* New York: Rawson Wade, 1979.

Friday, Nancy. *My Mother, My Self.* New York, Delacorte Press, 1977.

Gagnon, John. *Human Sexualities.* Glenview, Calif.: Scott Foresman & Co., 1977.

Goldberg, Herb. *Hazards of Being Male.* New York: Signet, 1976.

_____. *The New Male.* New York: William Morrow Co., 1976.

Gordon, Thomas. *Parent Effectiveness Training.* New York: Wyden Books, 1970.

James, Muriel, and Jongeward, Dorothy. *Born to Win: Transactional Analysis with Gestalt Experiments.* Reading, Mass.: Addison-Wesley, 1971.

Jourand, Sidney. *Transparent Self.* New York: D. Van Nostrand Co., 1971.

Kaplan Singer, Helen. *The New Sex Therapy.* New York: Brunner-Mazel, Inc., 1974.

Masters, William, and Johnson, Virginia. *Human Sexual Inadequacy.* Boston: Little Brown & Co., 1970.

_____. *Human Sexual Response.* Boston: Little Brown & Co., 1966.

_____. *The Pleasure Bond.* Boston: Little Brown & Co., 1975.

Miller, Sherod, Nunnally, Elam, and Wackman, Daniel. *Alive and Aware.* Minneapolis: Interpersonal Communication Programs, Inc., 1975.

Morgan, Marabel. *The Total Woman.* Old Tappan, N.J.: Fleming H. Revell Co., 1973.

O'Neill, Nina, and O'Neill, George. *Open Marriage.* New York: M. Evans & Co., 1972.

Peele, Stanton. *Love and Addiction.* New York: Taplinger Co., 1975.

Satir, Virginia. *Peoplemaking.* Palo Alto, Calif.: Science and Behavior Books, Inc., 1972.

_____. *Conjoint Family Therapy.* Palo Alto, Calif.: Science and Behavior Books, Inc., 1967.

Sheehy, Gail. *Passages: Predictable Crises of Adult Life.* New York: E.P. Dutton and Co., 1976.

Slater, Phillip. "Sexual Adequacy in America," *Earthwalk.* New York: Doubleday & Co., 1974.

Stevens, John. *Awareness.* Moab, Utah: Real People Press, 1971.

Toffler, Alvin. *Future Shock.* New York: Random House, 1970.

Zibergeld, Bernie. *Male Sexuality.* Boston: Little Brown & Co., 1978.

Acknowledgments

Over the seven-year evolution of this book, many people have influenced and contributed to my developing manuscript, from its original conceptualization through its many changes to its present form at first printing.

To start, I would like to thank Donald McKillop, Ph.D., for all his help and guidance when I was in graduate school. During that early period, Ronald Lempke, Ed.D., John James, M.A., and Muriel James, M.A., played an important role in developing my early models of couple communication patterns.

I also want to express my great appreciation to Tom Lowry, M.D., and Thea Lowry, M.A., for all their help and knowledge in training me to become a sex therapist and teacher.

Other people who played an early role in this book's development were Janet Dombrower, M.S., Elizabeth Hubrick, M.S.W., Mary Mullen, M.S., Allure Jeffcoat, M.S., and Virginia Satir, M.S.W.

Through the book's entire development, the following people made major contributions in various ways through their emotional support, feedback, and guidance. All of these people are or were part of the staff of Relationship Counseling Center, Walnut Creek, California: my partner, Michael Tobin, Ph.D., Sheilah Fish, M.A., Wes Laccoarce, M.S., Janet Forman, M.A., Joan Martin, M.S., Bonnie Cameron, M.A., Teresa Welborn, D.A., Renee Baron, M.A., Dennis Lees, M.S.W., Philip Manfield, Ph.D., Hank Visscher, M.A., Anthony Newey, Ph.D., Stephen Polsky, Ph.D., Michael Levin, M.D., and Marilyn Hanson, M.A.

The editorial staff who contributed to the creation of this book is headed by Carol Ball, my secretary, advisor, editor. I also want to express my gratitude to Ken Jones, M.S., and Hal Bennett for all their help in the rewrites and editing. I want to thank my typist,

Chris Pegan, for her efforts. My appreciation goes to the staff at West Coast Print Center and to Linda Moore for getting this book to the public in its initial form.

Special thanks go to Mae Keyson McAuley, Ph.D., and George McAuley, M.D., for their support, encouragement, and assistance in getting this book published.

In conclusion, I want to thank all my friends and relatives for their support and encouragement throughout the development of this book. I particularly want to thank the three most important people in my life. Without the support and love of my wife, Debra, the writing of this book would not have been possible. She has let me experience the reality of my ideals and has shown me that the intimacy I speak of can become something other than a theoretical concept. I want to express thanks for all the love, support, and encouragement that my mother, Edith Beaver, and my brother, Robert, have given me throughout my professional career and, especially, during the writing of this book.